BLACK PREACHING
Select Sermons in the Presbyterian Tradition

Black Preaching

SELECT SERMONS
IN THE
PRESBYTERIAN TRADITION

Edited by
ROBERT T. NEWBOLD, JR.

THE GENEVA PRESS

Philadelphia

Scripture quotations from the Revised Standard Version of The Holy Bible, Old Testament Section, Copyright 1952; New Testament Section, First Edition, Copyright 1946; New Testament Section, Second Edition, © 1972 by the Division of Christian Education of the National Council of the Churches of Christ in the U.S.A. Used by permission.

BOOK DESIGN BY DOROTHY ALDEN SMITH

Published by The Geneva Press®
Philadelphia, Pennsylvania

PRINTED IN THE UNITED STATES OF AMERICA

Library of Congress Cataloging in Publication Data

Main entry under title:

Black preaching.

CONTENTS: Adair, T. D. Jesus Christ, the same yesterday, today—forever.—Cozart, L. S. The missing ingredient.—Udoh, E. B. Having no one [etc.]
    Includes index.
    1. Presbyterian Church—Sermons. 2. Sermons, American—Afro-American authors. I. Newbold, Robert T., 1920–
BX9178.A1B55   252'.05'1   77–4015
ISBN 0–664–20779–0
ISBN 0–664–24323–1 pbk.

Dedicated to
RUTH HILL
IRENE JOHNSON NEWBOLD
ROBERT THOMAS NEWBOLD, SR.
*who acquitted themselves well
as stand-ins for God*

CONTENTS

ACKNOWLEDGMENTS

The acknowledgments that follow are not listed perfunctorily or because "it is the thing to do." They are here because the editor made the preparation of this book a team effort.

The seminal idea of this publication was conceived in the mind and spirit of J. Oscar McCloud, General Director, Program Agency, The United Presbyterian Church in the United States of America. He has given generously of his time, encouragement, and counsel.

The preachers—lay and clergy—who wrote, submitted, and revised the sermons in this anthology have, by their cooperation, earned my profound gratitude.

An advisory committee assisted me in carefully reading the sermons submitted, in making helpful suggestions regarding revisions, and in formulating hard decisions regarding substantive changes. The members of the committee are:

St. Paul Epps, Executive Director, National Committee on the Self-Development of People, The United Presbyterian Church in the United States of America

Emily Gibbes, Associate General Secretary, Division of Education and Ministry, National Council of Churches

W. Eugene Houston, Assistant Secretary and Eastern Area Representative, Board of Pensions, The United

9

Presbyterian Church in the United States of America

James Reese, Coordinator of Professional Development, Vocation Agency, The United Presbyterian Church in the United States of America

Gladys Strachan, Women's Program, Ministries with the Laity, Program Agency, The United Presbyterian Church in the United States of America

Edgar Ward, Associate General Director for Personnel Services, Vocation Agency, The United Presbyterian Church in the United States of America

The secretaries who invested a great deal of their time in typing drafts of the manuscript, and had special interest in this effort, are Marian Liggins, Albertina Jones, and Joyce E. Evans. I remain greatly indebted to them.

Dr. William P. Thompson, Stated Clerk, General Assembly, The United Presbyterian Church in the United States of America, encouraged and supported me in this project. Mildred Wager, Janet Penfield, and Pamela Wells brought years of experience and skill to their proofreading task. Cassandra Norman provided the index.

Three persons created an atmosphere in our home wherein I could do research, write, edit, and meditate. They are Anne, Denise, and Gregory. I hereby acknowledge appreciation for their understanding and cooperation.

INTRODUCTION

In this book, something of the richness and power of black preaching is preserved for the inspiration and edification of the whole church of Christ. The preachers, through whom God speaks and whose sermons are offered here, represent a wide span of age and experience. Their roots are in Africa and various sections of America. This group of men and women includes active pastors; pastors technically inactive in the church, although certainly active in the work of the Lord; judicatory executives; seminary professors; former Moderators of the General Assembly; and lay preachers.

Black Presbyterian preachers often find themselves in the middle of a controversy. Some of the white preachers within the denomination question their homiletical ability. Many black clergy, colleagues outside the denomination, feel that black Presbyterian preachers stand out as scholars, Biblical interpreters, and lecturers, but not necessarily as preachers. Such judgments were primarily occasioned by the fact that white questioners insisted on judging black preaching by white standards. Further, a number of brothers and sisters concluded that no authentic black preaching occurs outside the black church.

The mutual error in both positions is reflected in the fixed assumption that there is only one way to preach. The sermons in this collection remind us that preaching cannot be judged by one method of preparation, content formula, and delivery style alone. The twenty-one messages reflect how God utilizes a variety of people as messengers.

This book is not an attempt to bring to the attention of the reading public all the best sermons by outstanding black Presbyterian preachers. That is too massive a task. Rather, these sermons are representative of the type of preaching being done in black Presbyterian churches today. The men and women who wrote them are among the best contemporary black preachers, though there are many others whose work is not included here.

The editor developed a tentative list of names based on his twenty-four years of listening to black Presbyterian preachers. This list was shared with members of the advisory committee, who used the following criteria in selecting and editing the material to be published:

1. The message had to be a sermon—that is, Biblically based. It should have been designed to improve the listener's relationship to God and to other human beings.

2. The sermon must have been delivered in a church worship setting, and "tested" for use and effect of metaphors, black Biblical interpretation, and the dialogue response.

3. The sermons must have dealt with some aspect of the black experience. That experience is basically one of oppression, with overtones of loss of spirit and of frustration with powerlessness.

We have outlined the background of the book and the process by which its contents were selected. This guide and the introductory statement before each sermon are intended to provide an appropriate context for the messages that follow. Thus, the reader is left to judge how well each sermon meets the criteria.

1
Jesus Christ, the Same Yesterday, Today—Forever

THELMA DAVIDSON ADAIR
New York, New York

Thelma Davidson Adair was born in Iron Station, North Carolina. She is the granddaughter and daughter of Baptist ministers. Three of her four brothers are graduates of Johnson C. Smith Theological Seminary. It is little wonder she is an effective lay preacher.

Ruling Elder Adair is the first black woman Moderator of the General Assembly of The United Presbyterian Church in the United States of America. The Presbytery of New York City proudly sponsored her candidacy for this office because of her thirty-five years of service in the Mt. Morris Church and leadership in the community. She organized the Sunday church school and Children's Center.

She was an Associate Executive Secretary, Department of Health, Education and Welfare, Board of National Missions; a member of the Board of Christian Education; and chairperson of the Special Committee on the Needs and Rights of Children. She is the immediate past national president of Black Presbyterians United.

Thelma Adair has served on the boards of trustees of a college, a university, a theological center, and a seminary. She has traveled in Africa, the Far East, the Middle East, and the Caribbean. She has lectured in a number of universities and colleges and served as adjunct professor in two theological seminaries.

She has a commanding platform and pulpit presence. Her thoughts are verbally driven home to her listeners on the crest of a salutary emotional experience. She often appears to be moved by the convictions reflected in her speeches and sermons. She, in turn, moves her listeners to deep reflection.

This sermon was preached in the National Presbyterian Church, Washington, D.C., January 2, 1977. It has subsequently been expanded and revised for inclusion in this anthology.

SERMON 1

We look to Jesus the pioneer and perfecter of our faith.

HEBREWS 12:2

Jesus Christ is the same yesterday and today and for ever.

HEBREWS 13:8

Christ is our heritage of the past, our reality of the here and now, and our future hope and promise. In the past week millions around the world celebrated the birth of Jesus. Persons of the highest worldly positions bowed and worshiped. The pews of the great cathedrals were filled. Those of the humblest estate came in reverence and worshiped. Many believers prayed from the simplest wooden benches. All humanity, believer and nonbeliever alike, paused for the birthday of the Prince of Peace.

This week marks the start of a new year. Though we are quickly thrust from this "wondrous birth" back into the world of change and decay, Jesus is the same every day. In the midst of this unchanging, often chaotic world, we find our stability in a changeless Christ. Jesus, the one on whom our faith depends from beginning to end, is with us. Thus we say confidently—"Emmanuel." It is this Jesus who gives us the continuity and strength to live the "todays" of our life.

If we keep a sense of the guiding presence of Christ in our minds, the stability we find in a changeless God, the paradox and the power of Christians and the Christian church become clear. We begin to understand that the church lives and operates in a three-dimensional religious reality of yesterday, today, and forever.

The record of yesterday, which we call history, grew from

14

writings like the Hebraic treatment of historical episodes in the Old Testament. This is the account of God's dealings with his chosen people. From this we become acquainted with the God who sent Abraham into a strange land. We learn of a Jehovah who sent Moses into Egypt to meet Pharaoh with the message, "Let my people go." We come face to face with the one who is described by Darius, Daniel's tormentor, as "greater than my God, for he has stopped the mouths of lions." Thus the Hebrew people saw clearly a direction to their lives under God. They saw God intervening again in a special way on their behalf. He sent his only Son, who in his life, teachings, resurrection, and church brought salvation, fresh meaning, and purpose to humankind. It does not surprise us then that the God who interacted with such might in the lives of the Old Testament leaders fulfilled his promise to humanity by sending us his only Son. And, it was this Son, of whom Paul wrote to the Hebrews saying: "We look to Jesus the pioneer and perfecter of our faith . . . who is the same yesterday and today and forever."

So, when we look to Jesus, the beginning and end of our faith, we see his sufficiency for both today and forever. For the problems we face today are the same as those our fathers and mothers, and many generations before them, faced. The tasks are not new. They are basically the same—whether today, or yesterday, or tomorrow. And it is Jesus who helps us face these problems. Yes, the sympathizing tear, the patience to fight, the courage to go on, the knowledge that we do not walk this road alone is the essence of a life of faith centered in Jesus.

Just as our personal faith is anchored in Jesus Christ, so is the corporate faith which is reflected in the mission and ministry of the church. For the church is his, not ours. It is his new creation. He is its foundation.

Indeed, the church is the body of Christ. It is composed of believers who are bound together by the conviction that they have been redeemed, born again, saved.

As Presbyterians we represent a branch of Christendom that has been designated the Reformed tradition. Our literal and spiritual forefathers found this "promise" theme in God's work. The opportunities for ministry, their deep spiritual commitment, and their response to God's Spirit led our church to follow Jesus in a special way. The result of all this was and is involvement in mission in many forms.

One of the areas of mission to which our church is addressing itself is the status of women. This concern cannot be confined to the ordination of women to the ministry, as profound as that question is. It is the broader problem of the acceptance of women as equals, the serious consideration of their ideas, their contributions, and acknowledgment of their strength in the life of the church. We must be aware that in the long history of our church there have been only two women Moderators of the General Assembly. As this relates to my own life and my desire to make a contribution, I am not unappreciative of my having been elected to be one of the two. However, the election of two women Moderators out of 188 who have held this office speaks for itself.

Our attention to the issue of basic justice for women cannot be limited to the United Presbyterian Church or to the United States. When we approach this issue universally, we are forced to divide the world into two separate areas. This is because the concerns of women in the United States and in Western Europe are different from those of Third World women. In the developing nations such notions as equal rights under the law, equal pay, inequities in the social security laws, the effect of the law on marriage, the family and divorce, are hardly priority concerns of these women enslaved by custom and tradition.

Many women of the Third World spend their lives in the fields, suffer malnutrition and cruel treatment, and have no access to education. The concerns of women in the United States and in the Third World are massively different, but the underlying thrust is the same. It is the quest for fulfillment, the recognition of personhood, and a consistent wish for self-development.

Our church must constantly seek to support this thrust. The church must again, as it did during the fight for civil rights, actively seek the disorder, the drastic social change which some social scientists predict will come from restructuring our society. Some Americans feared the social chaos which they were certain would follow the disruption of a highly profitable societal and economic slave structure. But with Jesus as the stabilizer, the constant in the changing world, the institution of slavery was overthrown. Today we rejoice in that event. With regard to women's rights, not just in the Western world, but around the globe, we will rejoice to see women free at last.

Another area of mission is minority education. Our church has a long history of working actively for racial and ethnic justice. At the close of the Civil War, the Presbyterian Church was a leader in providing educational and religious training for the newly freed slaves. Dedicated and consecrated men and women from scores of local churches across this country went south and invested their lives in this cause. My father, his sister, and almost every member of my family were educated in this way.

I am an alumna of our Presbyterian Church-related schools. Once these institutions numbered in the hundreds. The cultural and spiritual influence upon the cities and towns where they were located was incalculable. The quality of education in those schools was higher, almost universally, than in the public schools. Many of them were human relations bridges between the black and white communities. Many students, parents, teachers, community leaders "joined" the Presbyterian Church because of its outstanding ministry of education. So, our church has written brilliant chapters in the annals of minority education.

Today there are only eight church-sponsored schools for minorities. The results of such a drastic reduction are not always obvious or measurable. However, we know that the need for quality education for the disinherited and the dispossessed is acute. There is a critical need for black clergy leadership in the United Presbyterian Church. And church membership growth in black Presbyterian churches is lower now than when these schools were open. To ignore these facts is, in my opinion, to ignore the heritage of our church. As I have traveled across this country as Moderator of our church I have been saying to congregations that we can ill afford to lose the last vestige of our glorious heritage in the area of minority education.

Another area of ministry is hunger. We cannot be "at ease in Zion" knowing that during the first quarter of 1975, 670,000 victims of hunger, or of hunger-induced disease, died. Members of the Christian community cannot take their commitment to Christ seriously, while complacently hearing the report that ten thousand hunger deaths occur in the world each day in the year. We cannot dismiss casually the triage theory, the "sorting out" principal, in which the belief is advanced that half of the world's hungry should be left to perish in order that another half may be fed and kept alive. We thank God for the fact that the church has been neither complacent nor casual concerning this international crisis.

Many of the Protestant denominations in the United States have taken official action calling for public policy changes on food and related issues.

If the church is to be true to the Christ, who is the author and finisher of our faith, it must continue to advocate for those state, national, and international actions that will provide that

no child will go to bed hungry;

no family will want for the next day's food;

no person's future or capacities will be stunted by malnutrition.

It was during the 187th General Assembly (1975) that our own denomination made hunger one of the church's major mission priorities and directed that a Hunger Fund be established to assist and direct food relief, development assistance, education and interpretation, life-style modification, and to influence public opinion.

This happened at the General Assembly in Cincinnati.

What is happening in the congregation where you worship regularly? What are you doing about "the inequalities and unjust structures" that cause starvation? What have you committed yourself to do about this massive crisis?

Jesus calls us to give ourselves in service to the needs of the poor. Listen!

> For I was ahungered, and ye gave me meat: I was thirsty, and ye gave me drink. . . . Lord, when saw we thee ahungered, and fed thee? or thirsty, and gave thee drink? . . . Inasmuch as ye have done it unto one of the least of these my brethren, ye have done it unto me. (Matt. 25:35, 37, 40)

Another concern of our church is the healing of the broken body of Christ. Each week many of us stand to affirm what we believe. One of the affirmations is the belief in the catholicity of the church.

"I believe in the holy catholic church." What this statement reflects is a concern for the whole, universal church. It indicates that we are committed to "a unitive and communal fellowship." And we are so committed because we believe in one God who is Lord and father of all. We believe that the Lord Jesus Christ, "the pioneer and perfecter of our faith," is the head of the church. In him, and by him, the church is one:

> For as the body is one, and hath many members, and all the members of that one body, being many, are one body: so also is Christ. For by one Spirit are we all baptized into one body, whether we be Jews or Gentiles, whether we be bond or free; and have been all made to drink into one Spirit. (I Cor. 12:12–13)

Witness to the reality of this oneness, however, is not only in a creed or a hymn. Rather, it is in our commitment and witness to God, whose son Jesus is the same today and forever. It is in our working together to heal the brokenness of the church, the body of Christ. It is in allowing ourselves to be used by the Holy Spirit to foster a spirit of goodwill among all persons regardless of theological differences.

Dean R. Hoge, in his book *Division in the Protestant House*, reminds us that

> The New Testament clearly condemns divisiveness among Christians. It holds up an ideal of unity of all Christians, be they Jew or Greek, male or female, slave or free. This ideal has been one source of Christianity's appeal over the centuries.
>
> Jesus opposed Jewish class distinctions and condemned the pretenses of the self-righteous who thanked God that they were not as other men. He ministered to the poor and outcast, and he used as an example a Samaritan who expressed human love across racial divisions. He opposed the exclusive national claims of both Jews and Romans. In the book of The Acts the Jerusalem church upheld an equality first of worldly goods and later of office and sacrament, defending its unity in Christ against the ethnic and class barriers of the surrounding culture.

And so we must witness to and defend our unity in Christ against "the ethnic and class barriers of the surrounding culture." We must continue to contribute to the Church of Christ Uniting and make significant investments of time and money in those activities witnessing to our oneness in Christ. When do we stop making this kind of investment? When there is demonstrable proof that the prayer of Jesus has been answered.

> Neither pray I for these alone, but for them also which shall believe on me through their word; That they all may be one; as thou, Father, art in me, and I in thee, that they also may be one in us: that the world may believe that thou hast sent me. And the glory which thou gavest me I have given them; that they may be one, even as we are one: I in them, and thou in me, that they may be made perfect in one; and that the world may know that thou hast sent me, and hast loved them, as thou hast loved me. (John 17:20–23)

These four concerns—justice for women, minority education, hunger, and ecumenism—are capstones of the church's ministry. And there are no simplistic methods and instant answers to the questions that are wedded to them. They call us to a long-term, expensive commitment that transcends our wisdom and resources. Doubtless there are those who have already concluded that these concerns add up to a hopeless situation. Is it really hopeless?

I spent last Christmas in Haiti with my daughter, son-in-law, and two grandchildren. My, that place was busy. Excitement was in the air. There, in that strange place, a busy part of the world, I heard a familiar voice. It came from a large amplifier outside the door of a record store. Mahalia Jackson was singing the lines we all have heard a hundred times. They are:

> A thrill of hope the weary world rejoices,
>   For yonder breaks a new and glorious morn;
> Fall on your knees, Oh, hear the angel voices!
>   O night divine, O night when Christ was born!
>   O night, O holy night, O night divine!

"A thrill of hope. . . ." That's it!

As we look to Jesus, the author and finisher of our faith, the same yesterday, today—forever, we recognize the complexity of the ministry that we are called to perform. But thank God we are also charged with a new and exciting thrill of hope.

2
The Missing Ingredient

LELAND S. COZART
Charlotte, North Carolina

Leland Cozart is one of the best lay preachers in The United Presbyterian Church in the United States of America. His deep religious commitment, meticulous preparation of sermons, ability to think clearly on his feet, and resonant, commanding voice have brought this reputation to this educator-preacher.

Cozart was born in North Carolina. His formal education was received at Biddle (Johnson C. Smith) University, Teachers College, and Harvard University.

He spent his entire professional life in education as high school teacher, principal, and for thirty-two years as president of Barber-Scotia College. During his tenure as president of Barber-Scotia College, he also served as secretary and treasurer of the Association of Colleges and Secondary Schools.

Before going to Barber-Scotia, Leland Cozart served as Executive Secretary of the North Carolina Teachers Association and editor of the *North Carolina Teachers Record.* He is also the author of *A History of the Association of Colleges and Secondary Schools; A Venture of Faith: History of Barber-Scotia College; Highlights of the Centennial Year—1967;* and *Critical Problems in the Education of Negroes.*

"The Missing Ingredient" provides the reader with the opportunity of obtaining a sample of Leland Cozart's style of sermon-writing. Unfortunately it does not provide a similar opportunity regarding his sermon delivery.

"I have carefully kept all these," returned the young man. "What is still missing in my life?"

MATTHEW 19:20 (PHILLIPS)

Then Jesus said to him: "If you want to be perfect, go now and sell your property and give the money away to the poor— you will have riches in Heaven. Then come and follow me!" The young man went away with a heavy heart, for he was very rich.

This dialogue between Jesus and a man who was in search of a richer, fuller life turns on a question leaping from the emptiness of the life of an otherwise remarkable person—a question as relevant in our day as at any time in the past. Indeed no man, except the Son of Man, has achieved the perfection that makes this question obsolete. Before we ponder it further, however, let us make one or two observations concerning this confrontation.

In the first place, Jesus shows no interest in entering into a philosophical discussion of goodness. He comes directly to the point and challenges the young man to a profound self-examination. Why do you come to me to talk about goodness? Only One is good. Furthermore, we are saved not by our goodness but by grace through faith. That which we truly need is offered by God in Christ.

Moreover, the clear implication is that God loves us not because we are good but because he is good. And although keeping the commandments is a basic requirement for the good life, there may still be a missing ingredient to the larger

24

freedom and the fulfillment of life at its best.

The second observation, measured by human standards, is that this young man was a remarkable person. Jesus himself acknowledged this when he said, "You lack one thing." The young man was possessed of rich potential. He was wealthy, yet unspoiled; his character record in keeping the commandments was exemplary. He knew his limitations and attempted to respond to the urge to fill with goodness the aching void of his life. He was young, not merely in years, but in dreams and visions. Generally speaking, we say: Young men dream dreams and old men see visions. The prophet Joel says it in reverse:

> Your old men shall dream dreams,
> and your young men shall see visions.
>   (Joel 2:28)

The prophet is saying that if the Spirit of the Lord is upon them, even our old men will keep the spirit of youth and continue to dream dreams; and even our young men of such a mind will have some of the vision and wisdom of age beyond their years. How applicable to this young man!

Yet Jesus looked him straight in the eye and said: "This is all very fine, but there is still a missing ingredient in your life. I must insist that you get rid of your stores of wealth, give the money to the poor, and then come and follow me."

Here the lines were drawn hard and fast. Here a moral dilemma projected itself in bold relief—on the one hand, total self-concern; on the other, total concern for others. To resolve the impasse called for total commitment to Christ. There the young man stands at the fork in the road of his destiny, before the blazing light of the moment of truth in his life, paralyzed with fear to attempt to solve the problem involving his wealth, unable to resolve his dilemma, except to be committed to and commanded by his Lord. So he attempts to absolve himself by running away. He leaves under the weight of a depressed spirit, perhaps never to return to witness the fact that Jesus had anxieties too, but they were not centered in himself. That Jesus wept over Jerusalem, prayed for his disciples, agonized in the

Garden of Gethsemane, and died on a cross, burdened with the sins of the world—sins on him, but no sin in him.

Furthermore, we can't derive some neat principle of procedure even from our deepest concerns which may be met with frustrations at their very source. The clue to the matter is not in the question we put to life, but in our response to the question life puts to us—the demand life makes upon us. We may come face to face with Jesus and yet not discover him. To discover him, as did the woman at Jacob's well, is to discover one's self. We may even recognize him as the revelation of God's love and fail to make him Lord of our lives. We may hail him as good Master and still refuse to obey him. We may proclaim him as the great physician and neglect to follow his prescription for spiritual health.

Let us suppose for a moment that the young man who approached Jesus with his question had been poor instead of rich. How would Jesus have answered him? I do not pretend to know, but one thing is certain. He would have answered in terms of the young man's need.

Here lies the crux of the whole matter: the searching significance of the missing ingredient is primarily individual. The besetting sin of one person may not be the major problem of another. The individual cannot develop his maximum potential or share in the redemptive work of Christ unless and until he has made him Lord of his life and accepted the ingredient of unconditional commitment by which his lesser problems are resolved as he grows in spiritual maturity.

So, if one confronts the Man of Nazareth today with the burning question leaping from his soul, "What is still missing in my life?" our Lord's answer will surely be in terms of that individual's need at that time.

To some he would say: Recapture simple honesty and integrity lest the light that is within you turn to darkness. To those who exploit the helpless, the lowliest, and the lost, his unanswerable challenge would come: Do unto others as though you were the others. Those who encourage or participate in lingering racism, he would warn: You are engendering a reaction of violence that even your favored situation cannot continue to cope with, especially when that violence is born out of desperation. For those who are consumed by hate, whether in retaliation or provocation, are under the judgment of death by their own decree. To many in high places and low who have embraced a new freedom which cannot possibly make free, the Master would plead, "Turn back, O man, forswear thy foolish ways," for history belies the fallacy of moral relativism and piles up mountains of evidence that all our skills are powerless to solve our problems, except as we are disciplined to deal with them in terms of moral value.

A professor at Drew University warns that the most serious situation facing modern society is not changing moral standards, but rejecting the idea of there being any moral standards to change.

Many a life self-destructs at this point, and many societies have gone to pieces by the same catastrophe. Our corporate creations cannot possibly escape the demands made upon individuals who compose them. Therefore, what is still missing with the individual does carry over to the group, even to the corporate state.

David Halberstam's book *The Best and the Brightest* presents a frightening picture of the spiritual chaos and political insecurity that threaten this nation. It shows with deadly connotations that in the period of the 1960's—an extraordinary confluence of time and men—we were led deliberately into a senseless war which took an inordinate toll of our spiritual and material resources, leaving death and decay that will mock us for time without reckoning.

Charles A. Reich in *The Greening of America* also takes a close look at our social scene when he says:

> The logic and necessity of the new generation—and what they are so furiously opposed to—must be seen against a background of what has gone wrong in America. It must be understood in light of the betrayal and loss of the American dream, the rise of the Corporate State of the

1960's, and the way in which that State dominates, exploits, and ultimately destroys both nature and man.

We should do well to spend more time trying to relate this dream to the Christian ethic as the saving grace for these times. The American dream from the beginning involved much more than a device for political determination; it was buttressed by moral and spiritual values.

An occasional battle cry is: We must tighten law and order. With this we would all agree. But as Fosdick once put it so forcefully:

> In the long run the law can get out of the people no more goodness than there is inside the people. The law is much like a pump, and the water it pumps is the intellectual, moral, and spiritual life of the people—no more, no less.

A long time ago Plato voiced the belief that men and societies should be judged by what they value most. To arrive at that insight demands a critical attitude toward practices as opposed to promises—practices overt and covert; shameful practices revealed by the widespread waves of greed and graft, of crime and scandals, most foul.

In the name of all that is holy, then, do we not want to restore the American dream? Do we not long to redeem the times that have caught many of our youth and fixed their strivings with new dreams devoid of saving ingredients? Is it not time that as individuals and as nations we cry out in deep humility and seriousness: What is still missing in my life?

Christ has the answer for each one of us. Christ is the answer! The supplier of our deepest need, individual or corporate; "pioneer of a new humanity." Our help in ages past, our hope for years to come!

3
Having No One

ENYI B. UDOH
Nigeria

"Having No One" was the first sermon Enyi B. Udoh preached in Ediene Parish of the Presbyterian Church in Nigeria. It was delivered after a civil war and a cholera epidemic had left evidence of their presence upon his people and their property. The objective of the young African preacher was, therefore, to encourage his listeners to renew their faith in God and their support of the church.

Udoh was ordained four years ago. However, he elected to prepare himself for more effective parish ministry by engaging in graduate study at Princeton Theological Seminary.

Following a year of academic work, he returned to pastoral duties in Nigeria, where he plans to demonstrate the impact the Christian ministry can make upon all facets of life.

SERMON 3

Wilt thou be made whole? The impotent man answered him, Sir, I have no man, when the water is troubled, to put me into the pool: but while I am coming, another steppeth down before me.

JOHN 5:6–7

A Typical Question. Does it make sense to ask a sick person, "Do you want to recover?" Is it the normal way to ask a drowning person who has just about a few seconds before ending his struggle with waves in the bottom of a sea, "Do you really need my help?" Imagine a first-aider questioning people who are involved in a car accident and bleeding profusely, "Do you guys really need an emergency service?" Or maybe we want to think of a scene in which a house was being ripped off by fire and trapping in children. Fortunately, a fireman happened to find his way through, but instead of rescuing the kids, he turned around to ask, "Do you kids want to escape the blaze?"

1. In spite of evidence—Well, Jesus' question to the paralytic was something of the sort: "Do you want to recover?" It is indeed surprising that Jesus still had to ask, "Do you?" in spite of available and convincing evidence. John, who probably was with Jesus at the pool, reports that he clearly saw the paralytic lying down there. And more, that Jesus was aware of his lengthy predicament. The sheep pool was neither a theater nor a football stadium. Rather, it served as what we might call a sick bay, with an unusual crowd. It was not the kind of crowd that gathered to listen to God's word or to be fed or to watch an artist perform. It was not a protest group demonstrating against a certain government policy. It was, in fact, a disabled crowd. As we say, "A weakling does not match his equal," or,

"He who cannot figure out the ugly look of the baby monkey when it is sick may try to look at a lemur."

2. In spite of the traditional healing system—The sheep pool healing system operated on a "first come, first served" basis, a situation that was bleak for people like the paralytic. Healing was based on self-effort. It became gradually clear after thirty-eight years that the paralytic would never make it. He simply couldn't move freely through the crushing crowd. As he put it, "While I am moving, someone else is in the pool before me." He became a victim of the community. All his struggles had so far been in vain since he managed to find his second home at the pool. The loss of a race can be disheartening, and the word "loss" itself is an unhappy one, either loss of property, loss of loved ones, loss of health or job. Many, if not all, did and still continue to feel the pangs of loss brought on us during and even after the Civil War. "Do you want to recover?"

A Crippling Evaluation. One obvious difference between the conditions surrounding a drowning person or an accident victim, on the one hand, and the paralytic, on the other, is the urgency involved with the former. We all have great obligation to accident victims whenever and wherever we happen to find ourselves in the scene. But the paralytic did not require emergency treatment. He had lived in that condition for years. Jesus' question, however, did not seem to impress the sick man. He might have thought it to be irrelevant to his condition. He therefore reformulated the question in silence and answered it aloud. He seemed to be saying, "Look, my man, my problem isn't recovering, and not even a question of do I want to." Healing does not occur as a miracle. One has to possess the necessary means—namely, someone. Maybe he, in fact, did not have relatives or friends around. Or maybe friends deserted him when his condition became worse or continued to remain the same. Maybe he did not, in fact, have someone who could accept, tolerate, and understand him in that condition. Maybe he needed friends like David and Jonathan or even the type of friends who brought their paralytic friend to Jesus (Mark 2:1–5). Not just anybody, but as he put it, "I have no one to put me in the pool when the water is disturbed." Yes, the right man at the right time. That, everyone needs today. Someone who really cares and is committed. Someone whose concern is not necessarily on the basis of reward. He was right. We say, "One who wins a case is surely the one who has people around." Or again, "A person who has no one hardly hears the rumor around his kitchen." Very often we tend to value a system, or institution, or wealth, or even position, more than we value human beings. The world is torn into bits, cities burst into flames, villages are reduced to a football field, hardship, misery, and violence—all these are the effects of disregard for human dignity. God grades people the highest of all the creatures, giving them dominion over them. God becoming man is a testimony of his true regard for all men. By identifying himself with us, the man Jesus becomes a symbol of judgment for those who treat human beings as objects.

Like so many persons in the world, and maybe some in the church, the paralytic lacks something important in his discussion with Jesus. He does not show any knowledge of his guest. Jesus Christ was like any other visitor who happened to pass through Bethesda. "Sir," the paralytic said. In spite of his ailment, the paralytic is polite. However, if Jesus' person, words, and acts were something of a mystery to his disciples, is it surprising that the sick man had no idea about the visitor from Nazareth? The twelve students were all wrong when the question, "Who do you say that I am?" came up (Mark 8:27ff.), until the Holy Spirit revealed him to Peter. The return from the war, for us, is a return to God and the knowledge of his Son, who continues to reveal himself every day. "Do you want to recover?" he says again to us.

A Typical Answer. The sick man had had his chance and he used it properly. He gave a brief commentary on his life's history. He did not see any light out of darkness. It was all hopeless because he lacked the real means of recovery—he had no one. Look at the patience of God as we see it in this story in the face of Jesus Christ.

The Lord tolerated the paralytic and had just enough time

to listen to a long autobiography. He endured the pain of being negated. In fact, of being underrated. Notice that Jesus' question was ignored. The paralytic probably thought any sensible person ought to realize that at the sheep pool any question ought to be addressed to having the means—not the will. How do you often feel when someone says "No" to you or your proposal? Maybe the sick man had this belief about himself and the environment and only expected someone like Jesus to conform. Maybe we expect God to conform to our wishes and expectations instead of "Thy will be done." Maybe we become annoyed with him after the crisis because he did not save us from the threats of war. Maybe our prayers have been the reverse of his will and glory. Then, we need to reexamine ourselves and confess our self-will to the Almighty Father.

Note next the change of speaker, the change of tone, and the change from question to command: "Rise," "Take up," "Walk," as though Jesus were saying: "What do you mean by having no one? Look at me! I am your someone. Up on your feet. Forget about the disturbing water, forget about having no one, and walk homeward." Friends, nothing is too ugly for God to look at, nothing so bad he cannot purify, nothing too difficult for him to handle if we can rely on him and listen to his commands to us each day and rise above the lowliness of sin into the joy of our Father. That which pulls us down, that which distorts our vision so we cannot see and fight against all unholiness, crimes, tribalism, violence, and distrust in our leaders is sin. As long as we live with it, the nation is going nowhere, and the church has failed in its duty.

But the love of God is so overwhelming that in spite of us, our limitations, our foolishness, he has sent his Son to the world to reclaim us and restore the whole universal order. Christ comes to us so that we might be able to go to him. To go to him is something of a process. It involves struggle to overcome all the forces that are against God. To walk with him is not easy. It costs so much. But it is not impossible, since his grace is sufficient for us. Sure, we can never make it unless he gives us the power and the courage to walk through life. Walking his way means going the way of the cross. It does not end by simply taking up our stretchers, but gradually involves taking up our own cross and bearing one another's burdens. It involves being able to testify to the wonderful work of Christ in our lives before traditions and institutions which themselves are in need of redemption. Do you want to recover? Then get up! Organize yourself and walk.

Conclusion. If the question surprised the paralytic, it is because it was the question from God himself. And God's word has never ceased to surprise sin-sick souls. His work in the world is a surprise. His coming in human form is a surprise. His transforming a sinner into a saint is a surprise. But it is a surprise that is all for the salvation of man, the dead being raised, as the thirty-eight-year-old paralytic begins to bounce about. Isn't that a miracle? What he did for the paralytic, and much more, can be done to us and has been done already on the cross. He's saying again to each of us, "I am your someone special."

4
On Being Faithful Stewards

ELLEN A. SANDIMANIE
First Presbyterian Church
Clayashland, Mo. Co., Liberia

Ellen Sandimanie is a native Liberian. She was educated at a mission school, Bromley, and Liberia College, which is now called the University of Liberia.

For thirty years the Reverend Mrs. Sandimanie worked for the city government, progressing to become the first woman to head the city government as Mayor Commissioner of the Commonwealth District, City of Monrovia, from 1970 to 1976.

Not only in government activities has Ellen Sandimanie made remarkable strides but also in the church. She was elected the first woman vice-moderator of the Presbytery of Liberia. She is the president of the Presbyterian Church Women of Liberia. The Reverend Mrs. Sandimanie presently serves as pastor in the city of Clayashland.

Mrs. Sandimanie says that this sermon, which was preached in First Presbyterian Church, January 25, 1976, is one of her favorites "even though it does not deal with the black experience as you know it in America. The black experience in Liberia does not involve the large extent of unusual relationships as it does in America, because this is an all-black country governed by black people. This is the black experience in Africa."

Moreover it is required in stewards, that a man be found faithful.

I CORINTHIANS 4:2

Christian Friends,

Greetings in Jesus' name.

Paul's letter to the church at Corinth was written for the purpose of correcting disorders that had arisen in the church and setting before the early Christians a standard of Christian conduct.

The theme of this epistle is "Christian Conduct" in relation to the church, the home, and the world.

Paul's letter speaks of many things affecting the church, but one of the things spoken of is stewardship. It is the subject we would like to consider this morning because this is the most important phase of our Christian lives.

Paul had completed his formal warnings against the parties in the church at Corinth. Now he turns to the responsibilities of those who are to teach. They are servants of Christ, not subject to the whims of anyone.

Every Christian is a minister of Christ, and the word "minister" means "one in the service of the State of God." Taking it as it is, we will confine ourselves to the latter, one in the service of God.

What does it mean by "being in the service of God"? How does one get involved or enlist in this service? and What is expected of one in this service?

Let us try to find the answers to these three important questions.

1. When we speak of the service of God, we mean the giving of oneself to all sorts of work from the most inferior to the most honored and exalted.

This means, then, that we as servants of God must be willing to do all kinds of work for God. To name a few, we are to start as sexton; we are to get involved in the Sunday school, the choir, youth movements whereby we can help in getting the wayward boys and girls off our streets; in all the organs of our church until we reach the lofty positions of elder and pastor. But these are not all. The most important aspect of this service is administering to the needs of others, such as our less-fortunate brothers, who have not had the privilege of hearing the good news of the gospel. Some of these are the people in Fansey Town, Gwee Town, and the other Preaching Stations which we have maintained in the Todee District area, where we also have maintained a Mission School for over twenty-eight years.

Christ stressed this when he said, "I was a stranger, and ye took me not in: naked, and ye clothed me not: sick, and in prison, and ye visited me not." The righteous Son of God concludes this, saying, "Verily I say unto you, Inasmuch as ye did it not to one of the least of these, ye did it not to me." And these shall go away into everlasting punishment: but the righteous into eternal life. This, my friends, is the service of God.

2. Our next question is: How does one get into this service? The moment we confess that the Lord Jesus Christ is Lord, thereby giving up of ourselves, our souls and our bodies, to be a reasonable, holy, and living sacrifice which is our reasonable service acceptable unto God, we are involved. By this we can say, "I am a soldier in the army of the Lord, I am to obey every command, do anything, or go anywhere in his service."

3. Our last question is, What is expected of one in his service? The answer we can sum up in one word: "Faithfulness." This is the first requirement in a steward, for he deals with what belongs to God, and as stewards we are to be faithful in the discharge of our functions. We are to do what is right and pleasing in the sight of God, regardless of public opinion. We might at times feel that the task is too great or the problems difficult to solve, but in every case all these matters will be made clear and open by God himself. You might ask why it is necessary to be faithful. We are to be faithful in order to surmount the attacks of the devil. When the Holy Spirit descended on the Day of Pentecost he created the church militant. He transformed a little group of men into a band of faithful stewards, with the task of spreading the good news at all times. This missionary character of the church is to always advance, and never to retreat, for its task here below is to proclaim God's word until he comes.

There will continue to be the attack and the counterattack between the faithful stewards of Christ and Satan.

All of us know that as soon as the Holy Spirit starts to manifest himself in our stewardship, the resistance of the opposing forces begins to operate. Any steward who is truly faithful must expect attacks from within and from without. And if we permit the satanic forces to hinder our stewardship, we are to ask ourselves whether we are really fulfilling the divine purpose for which we were called by God or whether we are compromising too much with the world that tolerates our indifference.

Jesus warned his disciples of this when he said: "Remember the word that I said to you, 'A servant is not greater than his master.' If they persecuted me, they will persecute you; if they kept my word, they will keep yours also." (John 15:20.)

Therefore, we as stewards must not become discouraged by the attacks of the devil. Instead, we are to become hardened and more determined to continue our faithfulness. We must remember that God has put us in the position of trustees and stewards. There is some service we can render according to such gifts as he has seen fit to give us, or according to such opportunities as he may send our way. Let us offer such service as is worthy to be done for its own sake and in the best interests of our fellowmen, as we are able to form right judgments concerning their interests.

Thus, to live and to serve as Christians, stewards and trustees, each in his private station, is to carry the spirit of Christian fellowship into life's ordinary places. Those who so live will also command the trust and respect of their fellowmen and the approval of God.

Let us from this day forward commit ourselves to faithful stewardship.

"Moreover, it is required in stewardship that a man be found faithful."

Unto God the Father, God the Son, God the Holy Ghost, be ascribed in the church all honor and glory, might, majesty, dominion and power, now, henceforth, and forever.

5
Top Value Stamp

WILLIAM S. MERCER
Radcliffe Presbyterian Church
Atlanta, Georgia

William Mercer has a penchant for attention-arresting sermon topics. They frequently prompt the question, "I wonder how he is going to deal with that subject." Also, he refuses to avoid controversial items. And a plea for social justice is very frequently heard in his messages.

"Top Value Stamp" must be placed in the context of this type of preaching ministry. It was delivered in Sisters Chapel, Spelman College, Atlanta, Georgia. Faculty and students responded affirmatively to his message.

Atlanta has listened to William Mercer's voice in song and sermon during the past twenty-three years. He has planned and presented many innovative and creative worship services in Radcliffe Church during this period.

This preacher was born in Providence, Rhode Island. His formal education was received in the Providence public schools, at Lincoln University, Pennsylvania, and at McCormick Theological Seminary.

Mercer's work in the church includes membership on the Advisory Board of Boggs Academy, fund-raising for the Support Agency of The United Presbyterian Church in the United States of America, and membership on various committees of the Presbytery of Georgia. He has made a significant investment of time in the National Association for the Advancement of Colored People, the Southern Christian Leadership Conference, the YMCA, Pineview Convalescent Home, and the Atlanta Police Department Chaplains Advisory Board.

Before accepting the call to his present pastorate, Mercer served as director of a larger parish, and as group worker in Chicago and Buffalo.

SERMON 5

So God created man in his own image; . . . male and female he created them.
. . . And God saw everything that he had made, and . . . it was very good.

GENESIS 1:27–31

As a widower, I find the business of shopping something that is very real for me. At some stores I still encounter trading stamps. I have been through S & H Green Stamps, Holden, and sometimes Top Value Stamps. These latter stamps interested me, particularly when I was thinking of "women's liberation" and black women's involvement, where values are concerned. I dare suggest that from the text emanates the idea that God's creation of male *and* female was very good. As James Weldon Johnson put it in his "Creation," God stepped back and admired his handiwork. He was proud of what he had wrought. Thus, in God's mind, male *and* female were "Top Value." The stamp of God's approval was not only on man but upon woman as well.

There is much pressure on the black woman of today as she struggles to identify. There is the "pull" to get her to affirm her independence and womanhood, something which a preponderance of black women have always been able to do. On the other hand, there is the "tug" of the gnawing doubt that she can ever escape from the age-old role of sex toy and often maligned helpmate of man; that her position is inescapable, her status irreversible. It is all a matter of perspective.

The story is told of a young college student who wrote her parents, to whom she had not even addressed a "gimme" letter for three months. It went like this: "Dear Mom and Dad, I'm

42

sorry not to have written for so long a time but I didn't want to worry you with my problems of the last months. First, there was a fire in the dorm and I suffered a concussion as the result of jumping out of a window to escape the flames. While I was waiting for an ambulance, a fine dude, a gas station attendant, was very kind to me, even to the extent of offering to let me share his apartment when released from the hospital, until the dorm was repaired. He is really a fine person and has really got a keen pad—it's all I could ask. Oh, yes, and you will soon be proud grandparents.

"Before I close, however, I want you to know: (1) There was no fire. (2) No special dude in my life, no concussion, and you are not becoming grandparents. It so happens, though, I got a 'D' in history and an 'F' in biology, and I just wanted you to see this in perspective."

So it is with the black woman—it is all in her perspective, according to how you perceive her status. Time was when a fable existed that the only truly free person in the South was the black woman. Some freedom, when it only gave her license to tread otherwise forbidden paths. That was an ersatz freedom and there surely exists no mourning over the loss of that kind of quasi-liberty.

As Christians we can be proud of the impetus given to women's true liberation long, so long ago. Set in motion by Jesus himself, it reverberates in the Pauline epistles, in both Colossians and Galatians. As proud as I am of its genesis *in* the church, I must confess chagrin over its lack of full implementation *by* the church. Women preachers today yearn for the Top Value Stamp which Jesus Christ issued, so long ago, but which is frequently denied them today. While there are churches that still debate the ordination of women, there are some that ordain them and yet deny them a forum. How in the name of heaven can we who call ourselves "like Christ" ignore the bent of his message and the lesson of his example?

Jesus regarded every person as an immortal soul. He emphasized the quality of mankind, *Homo sapiens,* the human species, in the sight of Almighty God. This fact forbids sex discrimination as well as racial discrimination. All artificial barriers are removed before God. This Jesus of cradle and cross granted a Magna Carta to women, establishing the right of all individuals to rise to their highest intellectual and spiritual levels. He recognized the needs of women as well as of men. He never approved evil or condoned civil or legal discrimination against them. Here again, women were stamped "Top Value" where the Master was concerned.

The Gospels record that: He heard the pleas of fathers *and* the pleas of mothers; the plea of a father whose son was an epileptic *and* he answered the plea of a Canaanite woman for her daughter. He heard the cry of a blind man, "Lord, that I may receive my sight," *and* he felt the touch of a poor, ill, superstitious woman on the hem of his garment. He responded to the distress of a Roman centurion whose child lay at death's door, *and* he had compassion on a widow whose only son had died. Yes, yes! This observant Christ recognized and commended the unselfish spirit of an impoverished widow, giving her all, as over against the ostentatious display of those who could have done more. Often it would appear that in his sight women were not only top value but the very apex of humanity. He often drew an analogy between a father's love and God's concern for his own. Yet when he used a scene from life to depict his agony over Jerusalem he chose the figure of speech of a mother hen brooding over her young.

Paul, in spite of being depicted frequently as a male chauvinist where leadership roles in church were concerned, in Gal. 3:28 specifically placed top value on women as well as on men when he wrote that there is no such thing as Jew and Greek, slave and freeman, male and female, "for you are all one in Christ Jesus."

Our Lord Jesus recognized the spiritual intelligence of women in the Mary and Martha story. There he gently reproved Martha: "Let her alone; she has chosen the better part" —food for the spirit, sustenance for the soul. And oh how he lifted woman up to the top rung when he rebuked his disciples in Simon's house when Mary Magdalene poured the precious attar on his head. With the one hundred percent assent of all present, Judas had put into words what they all were thinking: "What a shameful waste!" (Reminds one of what some congregations say about what is too good for the parson.) At that moment Jesus made the sweeping statement that wherever the gospel should be preached, her act would be memorialized.

One of the outstanding events in this chronicle of "woman raising" events in our Lord's life has been considered by Biblical scholars to be out of place in John 8. They put it in a separate chapter and suggest that the most ancient witnesses do not even carry its record. But they do not deny its possible authenticity nor its being totally in character with Jesus. You know the story well; how some doctors of the law and Pharisees sought to put Jesus on the "hot seat," between the devil and the deep blue sea. Interrupting his teaching in the Temple, they brazenly brought the woman, allegedly caught in the very act of adultery. Moses, they insisted, said stone such. What do you, O wise Rabbi, say? Seeming to be in a quandary, Jesus doodled in the sand. Can you not imagine them pestering him, as a boy who thinks he has won a bet, or has a game won in checkers, shouts: "Move, move! What say? What say?" Without doing them the honor of seeing what they presumed would be a hangdog, defeated look on his face, he softly said, "Let him who is without sin . . . be the first to throw a stone." I dare to suggest that the inference was that they could not even honestly say they were not guilty of the *same* sin, perhaps with the *same* woman. Reminds one of the apocryphal book, Daniel and Susanna. Get an old Bible or the unabridged New English Bible and read it. But Jesus did not just leave it there. Upon addressing the question to the woman, "Where are your accusers?" and being told they had departed, he said, "If they do not condemn you neither do I. Go and sin no more."

In this incident our blessed Lord had, without a doubt, placed his stamp of Top Value on woman. There was no lowering of standards but an abolition of dual standards, one for men and another for women. Rather, he applied the same standard to both, irrespective of sex or status. He did away with that worst kind of discrimination, the protection of a group by applying a higher standard to them than we are willing to adopt for ourselves. To this day the "Johns" go scot-free while the ladies of the evening are hounded and prosecuted. Women sell —men buy. Who is guiltier? Briber or bribee? Jesus seems to be saying, "They are equally guilty."

Let us here be reminded that they go together, male and female, as the old song went: "Love and marriage go together like a horse and carriage." God's Top Value stamp is upon male *and* female, or vice versa.

Jesus acknowledged and affirmed women's spiritual worth. It was to the woman at the well that he gave his first clear proclamation that he was the Savior. It was also to her that he made that tremendous pronouncement which at once delocalized, denationalized, deracialized, *and* desexualized God. He said to her, "God is a spirit and they who worship him must worship him in spirit and in truth."

God began the trend: male and female he created them; Jesus institutionalized it. Perhaps someday, someday, we shall appreciate, fully, that God has put his stamp of Top Value, on man *and* woman.

6
Beyond Ourselves

BARBARA CAMPBELL
Synod of Red River
Presbyterian Church U.S.

Barbara Campbell enjoys the distinction of being the first, and only, black woman to serve as moderator of a synod in the Presbyterian Church in the United States. Before this, she was elected delegate to the Fifth Assembly of the World Council of Churches. She has served on various committees of her denomination. Also, her voice is heard in many pulpits throughout the church.

Ms. Campbell was born in Houston, Texas. She studied at Texas Southern University and Tuskegee Institute. After graduation she became a teacher in her native state, and was subsequently employed as a chemist in a nationally known laboratory. In 1975 she was selected one of the Outstanding Secondary Educators in the United States. She is the Associate General Director of the Synod of Red River, Presbyterian Church in the United States.

"Beyond Ourselves" was preached in the Pioneer Church. The objective was to encourage this small, struggling congregation to recognize and decide that the focus of its ministry must always extend beyond itself. This, indeed, is a reminder that all congregants need to hear and heed.

Then Jesus beholding him loved him, and said unto him, One thing thou lackest: go thy way, sell whatsoever thou hast, and give to the poor, and thou shalt have treasure in heaven: and come, take up the cross, and follow me.

MARK 10:21

Man is basically good. A young man came to Jesus wanting to know how he could inherit eternal life. He had kept all the commandments. He had been a good son, husband, father, neighbor, and an outstanding citizen in his community. He had observed all these things from his youth. But he had the feeling that something was lacking! Something more was needed for him to inherit eternal life. So he came to Jesus for the answer.

Jesus said to him: "You lack one thing; go, sell what you have, and give to the poor, and you will have treasure in heaven; and come, follow me." This the young man could not do, so he went away sorrowful.

Most of us are like the young man. We lack some one thing that keeps us from going beyond ourselves and becoming the Christian we ought to be. Sometimes it's our possessions, our jobs, our families, our social life that keeps us from doing the will of God. What is the will of God? We are told, "Go into all the world and teach the gospel." Come see, go tell, is the mission of the Christian church.

In her book *Beyond Our Selves*, Catherine Marshall, widow of Peter Marshall, a Presbyterian minister, says: "In order to follow the will of God in His plan for our lives, we must work out a plan for 'ego slaying.' "

How do we go about doing this? We must try to look at

48

ourselves as God looks at us. We must ask ourselves the following questions:

1. Can we see the limitation of self-centered living and the danger of it in every way?
2. Can we accept by faith that God hears us and will lead us to the next action to change our lives?
3. Can we accept the fact that there will always be a crisis or a series of crises in our lives, and with God's help we can live through them step by step?
4. Every day of our lives we shall still have to choose between selfishness and unselfishness. Can we make the choice?

If we can do a bit of ego-slaying, we can get beyond ourselves and do God's will in the world today.

The Christian church in its early days grew in numbers and in influence, because God used the testimonies of men and women who had something to say about Jesus. What they had to say was that this Jesus, who had died on a cross, was alive and spiritually present every day to the disciples. And they proclaimed everywhere they went, with enthusiasm and conviction, the good news of the gospel. It was, to them, the thrilling and exciting story of how life had been changed. And how they had been changed for life.

They could no more keep silent than a flower can withhold its fragrance or the sun keep back its light. The power that had made them different, they said, was available to anyone who would believe. Sin could be forgiven. Christ could come into human life to change natures and dispositions, to change moods and temperaments, to banish fears and worry. Also, he can remove shame and guilt, provide a new dynamism, new purpose in life, new joy, and a peace that nothing could destroy.

The early disciples were thrown into prison. They were persecuted, boycotted, hounded from place to place. Yet thousands joined their fellowship and discovered the truth they were proclaiming and found life becoming a new and thrilling experience. Surely they had found a life beyond themselves.

How does one attain the true Christian worth? How is one able to live beyond himself or herself? First, one must examine his or her life and remove from it all unworthy thoughts and deeds. Our tendency is to be overcritical, jealous, given to harsh and hasty judgments, self-centeredness, cheating and lying. To face up to ourselves in confession is healing, provided we move on to forgiveness and do not wallow in our wrongdoing. We must clean our minds of the thought of wrongdoing and fill our minds with the Spirit of God.

In his book *The Cross and the Switchblade*, the Reverend David Wilkerson indicates how he went beyond himself into the gangland scene in New York City. He said: "From the beginning I was directed by the Holy Spirit. I heard a voice and went out, even as Abraham went 'not knowing whither.'"

There are so many people we could mention who have gone forth and done more than was necessary. They have used their time and their talents. They have done so much for others without a thought of themselves. These people were not looking for fame and fortune, but only to serve God through helping their fellowman.

When I say these things I think of people like Albert Schweitzer, Booker T. Washington, George Washington Carver. I also think about those dedicated, hardworking Christians in the Missouri Delta. They are a part of the Task Force on World Hunger. This ecumenical group of men and women have been living and working with the people of the Missouri Delta since 1965. They have not only helped these poor people in this farming country to seek the usual state and federal aid, but they have established a self-help program. They have opened a credit union, a grocery store, a health advisory center, a legal assistance program, training programs, and are in the process of developing a comprehensive rural economic development operation. This small group of dedicated people is doing so much to help thirty thousand poor people. And as they develop programs and teach skills, they then can move on to new proving grounds and leave the people of this community to carry on for themselves.

Why do I mention these things to you at Pioneer Church? I think Pioneer Church has a proving ground right here in this community. You have already made a good start in extending yourselves beyond the boundaries of your church. You are already in the field, helping those in your community to help themselves no matter what faith they may be.

I say to you that progress is often slow and the race is not always won by the swift, but by the diligent. I marvel in your desire to minister to your community. I ask God to give you renewed vigor when you are tired, so that you will continue to go forward. I feel confident that you dedicated Christians will not let Pioneer Church die.

7

A Great Responsibility

LLOYD GREEN
St. James Presbyterian Church
Greensboro, North Carolina

Lloyd Green moved from the campus of Johnson C. Smith Theological Seminary in Atlanta, Georgia, to the manse of St. James Presbyterian Church of Greensboro, North Carolina, in a relatively short period of time. The transition from student leader to church pastor was brief but successful.

The preaching ability of this young theologian is one of the reasons why the congregants called the then recent seminary graduate to be their pastor. It is also one of the reasons why members and friends crowd into the sanctuary of this historic North Carolina church.

Lloyd Green was born in Jenkinsville, South Carolina, where his father is a brickmason and his mother is a teacher in the public school system. He is an alumnus of Johnson C. Smith University.

This young pastor joined Whitehall African Methodist Episcopal Church at an early age. He served there as an usher and as president of the junior church department. Sometime later he became the assistant superintendent of the Sunday church school. During his undergraduate study Green elected to transfer his denominational membership to The United Presbyterian Church in the United States of America.

These experiences influenced Lloyd Green to make a decision to become a minister. His description of this impact is: "Because of my active involvement in the church and because of my sincere conviction to try to reach out and help others, I decided that I should become a minister."

"A Great Responsibility" was preached in the St. James pulpit. In the sermon, this young preacher was clearly attempting to have his parishioners recall and face up to their responsibilities as Christians.

And I said unto the nobles, and to the rulers, and to the rest of the people, The work is great and large, and we are separated upon the wall, one far from another.

NEHEMIAH 4:19

Albert R. Johnson, writing in his book *Responsibility in Modern Religious Ethics,* says in the opening paragraph that the "language of morality is fickle." The words with which one generation will praise or blame, commend or condemn, may sound dull or even comical to their children.

Some of you in this sanctuary this morning can remember when words like "propriety," "piety," and "prudence" commanded a degree of respect as standards of moral excellence. Not any more. To be labeled as a pietistic person is to be disgraced in many circles of our society. Even the word "virtue," a word used in the past to describe a good person, is no longer the great word it once was.

But that is the way it is with words. When certain words lose their force, other words appear to take their place in the "lexicon of morality." One of these new words, those new arrivals, is the word *responsibility.*

The respectable person is the *responsible* person. The obedient person is now the *responsible* person.

The late President John F. Kennedy talked about it when he said, "Ask not what your country can do for you, ask what you can do for your country." In other words Kennedy was saying, we have a *great responsibility* to our country, and not the other way around.

One does not have to look very far to find a Biblical illustration of this point:

Nehemiah was a cupbearer in King Artaxerxes' army. The story has it that one day Nehemiah is visited by some friends from his native Jerusalem. He wants to know how things are going in his homeland. They report to him that things never looked so bad. The wall that had surrounded their city is no more. The people are hungry and in want. Nehemiah loved his people. So he goes and cries to the Lord and asks the Lord to forgive the sins of his people. But, he can't stop here because Nehemiah, by his nature, was a man of action. He asks the king: "Sir, would it be possible for me to go back home for just a little while?" "Go back and do what you have to do, Nehemiah," the king consents. Nehemiah goes back home and by night he surveys the damage to his city. It's worse than he originally thought. There is hunger, destruction, and devastation.

It was a great sacrifice on his part, because, you see, Nehemiah was "well fixed." He was the king's cupbearer—an important and influential position. But Nehemiah felt the great trouble and shame of his countrymen in Jerusalem. Finally, after surveying all of the damage that had been done, Nehemiah says to his people, "Let's rise up and build it back. We can do it."

One day while out on the wall, he reminded the people that the work was great and large and they were separated upon the wall. "We can't even see one another," Nehemiah said, "but each one of us is *responsible* for the building of the wall. It can't be built by a few. All of us must do our part. If we are attacked, don't worry—our God will fight for us."

Responsibility—It's one word that all of us must reckon with. One word that we've got to come to grips with; you can't get around it. It's one word that the church has to come to grips with. It's the word *to St. James—RESPONSIBILITY.*

And, oh how we've been defaulting lately! But this morning

I want to discuss three areas of *responsibility* that we as a church need to be reminded of:

1. We have a *great responsibility* to fashion the social climate in which we live. For example: I was interested in reading the account of a recent city council meeting held in Greensboro. The mayor's agenda item was a proposed massage parlor. The writer of the article let it be known that preachers were those who were most opposed to its operation. And the reason the clergy gave was that "the *parlor* would lead to a breakdown of morality in young people." Now, to be sure I don't condone the massage parlor. But to blame the operator of a massage parlor for the breakdown of morality is the *height of stupidity.*

The real reason, the real reason for the breakdown of morality in a society can be traced primarily to only one social unit, and that unit is called THE FAMILY.

George A. Kelly wrote a book called *The Christian Role in Today's Society.* In his book he states, "All of the basic ingredients required for a civilized society should be found in a good Christian home." "Usually," he says, "it is in the family where the child first gains from his mother and father the first dim reflection of the love which God holds for him, a love which has *his* welfare as its only purpose."

"It is in the home," he says, "where a child learns those virtues of faith, hope and charity, which he will carry to the end of his days. Inside the family circle, he may be encouraged to develop habits of thoughts and action which may make him a saint. Or he may learn other things, habits of selfishness, resistance to lawful authority, submission to any impulse which may strike him—which may well prove his undoing when he passes into adulthood."

"Children raised as saints or sinners inside the family are likely to remain saints or sinners until the end of their days."

But Kelly goes on. He states, "There are three ingredients to having a successful Christian family." Listen to them, parents and young people: *Understanding, acceptance,* and *inspiration.* Parents who are motivated by a strong Christian love for their child do not seek to make him something *he is not* or *cannot be*. They strive to understand all the factors that go into his personality and recognize that his native intelligence and talents are, above all, a gift from God. They accept him for himself alone, and with that in view, they inspire him to make the most of what he has. In everyday terms, parents don't hold a grievance against their daughter because they wanted a son. When parents are motivated by Christian love, they don't ridicule their son because he likes electronic equipment better than baseball. When parents are motivated by Christian love, they do not discourage their children from pursuing their goals because they want to be grandparents. When parents are motivated by Christian love, they respect the child's right to grow in his own way and they inspire him to do so.

But you say, "Rev. Green, I thought that you were talking about the *responsibility* of the church." I am. For I would submit to you that until the church begins to take its *responsibility* more *seriously*, there will be a decline in Christian families. For it is the church which has the *responsibility* to show people the Christian way to act and think. Not only the little ones, but the big ones too.

Yes, we have a *responsibility* to nurture the little ones; but an even greater *responsibility* to mama and daddy.

Yes, the church has the *responsibility* to fashion the social climate in which we live. But the records would indicate that in the social unit called the family, the church has not reached its goal.

2. But that is not the only *responsibility* that I believe the church has in this day and time. I believe firmly that the church has a *responsibility* to speak out in the political arena of our nation and our world.

But you say, "Rev. Green, I thought church and state were separate." Well, anyone who is a student of the American scene can see that is not true anymore. Murray Stedman, in his book *Religion and Politics in America,* says that it is unfortunate that the churches have not taken a judgmental role in the political life of our nation and the world; for, compared to other institutions, the churches have a greater sense of moral awareness, an ability to grasp the moral implications of great issues. Moreover, the churches and their leaders have a greater sense of perspective that is essential to making sound judgments.

There are those who would debate those statements, but I firmly believe that the church can no longer ignore political and social injustice. To expose these injustices may cause division and pain; but to ignore them will result in the destruction of the church as an instrument of God's will.

For example: I think the church has got to keep reminding the politicians of our nation that we can sit where we want, but we cannot pay for the meal. I think the church has the *responsibility* to keep reminding the political arena of this nation and this world that people need jobs! People need hope! And only through the political order can people get jobs and see their hopes renewed.

The older I become, the more I become convinced that the church must stand behind what it says are its convictions; what it says were its founding principles. Anything less than that results in an abdication of its responsibility.

3. There is one final *responsibility* that the church has. We who are members of God's church have the *responsibility* to tell others about the love and forgiveness of our God.

St. James got sidetracked somewhere. I am not sure where; perhaps it came when those who promoted the idea of sin came to dominate our religious scene. Perhaps they drove home the point so hard and cutting that many were turned off by the church. But you know the fact is, much of what they said was true.

We are sinners. We do wrong. We hurt others; sometimes we do it deliberately. We see somebody down and we try to step on him.

One Biblical writer says, "In sin was I born and in sin did my mother conceive me." Isaiah says, "All we like sheep have gone astray." But what those who promoted the idea of sinful man failed to tell was that we have a God who loves and forgives us. According to James F. Colaianni, in his book *Sunday Sermons*, "There are no exclusions here; black or white, red or yellow, rich or poor, or middle-class, native, immigrant or refugee, high and mighty or low down trodden, famous or infamous. All of us were covered when Jesus died on the Cross."

"Everyone with cancer or arthritis or migraine headaches or withered limbs was included. Everyone who dreads the dawning of a new day, or is depressed, or is bent low with guilt over some past event was included. Everyone who is overwhelmed with anxiety about the future was included. Everyone whose soul cannot rest because of an intense hatred was included. Everyone who is victimized by slavery to some awful habit was included." The church has the *great responsibility* to tell everybody about the love and forgiveness of our God.

Hear finally my text: "And I said unto the nobles, and to the rulers, and to the rest of the people, The work is great and large, and we are separated upon the wall, one far from another. In what place therefore ye hear the sound of the trumpet, resort ye thither unto us: our God shall fight for us." *What a great responsibility we have!*

8
God's Trombones
and Their Interpreter

WILLIAM LLOYD IMES
Dundee, New York

William Lloyd Imes's ministry spanned forty-four years. He was ordained by the Presbytery of Elizabeth on May 3, 1915. His first pastorate was at the Bethel Chapel of the Crescent Avenue Presbyterian Church in Plainfield, New Jersey, which he served until 1919, when he was called to the Lombard Central Church in Philadelphia. He served there until 1925, and was called to the St. James Presbyterian Church in New York City, where his influence is still felt.

In 1914 St. James had moved from downtown to West 137th Street. Under Mr. Imes's leadership it quickly outgrew these facilities and in 1927 moved to its present location at 141st Street and St. Nicholas Avenue. When he left in 1943, it had the largest membership of any black Presbyterian church, then or now—almost three thousand members. He was in great demand as a speaker in all churches and particularly in the Episcopal parishes of Harlem.

Mr. Imes was president of Knoxville College from 1943 to 1947. He then served as Associate Secretary of the New York State Council of Churches for Social Action until retirement in 1956. He then exercised a labor of love, first at his alma mater, Fisk University, as Visiting Dean of the Chapel, 1956–57, and then in the same position at Dillard University, 1958–59.

Imes was greatly influential as a catalyst for the integration of stores on Harlem's 125th Street. He joined Adam Clayton Powell and the Reverend John Johnson on the picket line as early as 1936. In a day when clergy gave lip service to liberalism and civil rights and blacks were rarely elected to office, Imes was held in high esteem across the church, but never elected to a significant judicatory position.

Born in Memphis in 1889, he represents the best of the past generations, as indicated by this sermon of more than thirty-five years ago. It has been published in his book *The Black Pastures* (Hemphill Press, 1957). Imes lives in retirement in Dundee, New York.

61

SERMON 8

So God created man in his own image, in the image of God created he him; male and female created he them.

GENESIS 1:27

I will arise and go to my father, and will say unto him, Father, I have sinned against heaven, and before thee.

LUKE 15:18

He being dead yet speaketh.

HEBREWS 11:4

One of the most fascinating volumes that has appeared in the history of American poetry, not to speak of that of the world at large, was that under the alluring title *God's Trombones,* written by James Weldon Johnson, and recaptured by him from the quaint originals of gifted and poetic souls in the far-off byways of Negro life in its varied American setting. Frankly, they are in many ways utterly in a class by themselves, for, outside of our own King James translation of the Scriptures, with frequent Old Testament stories and homilies, and some in the New Testament, cast in poetic form, there has been little if any attempt of the poem-sermon type, either in folk history or literary retelling. We are therefore all the more indebted to this great American of African tradition for his simple and beautiful rendering of this haunting music of sermons, based upon Scriptural narratives for the most part, and without dialect, without caricature, without any artifice whatever of the cheap or sensational sort. Mingled together in deft and ingenuous pattern are both the lyrical and the dramatic. Age-old reflections of profound insight are there, and bold realism without crudity, and imagination without flippancy. Perhaps the severest test of these poem-sermons would be their impact upon the minds of people who have known something of America's backwoods and camp-meeting religious traditions.

Wherever this has been observed, they ring true, and there is not one false or hollow note. They tell the Negro's deep interest in timeless truths of life and faith, of duty and destiny, of character and conduct. And they do this through the idiom of the classic English of the King James Version. Our poet himself tells in his foreword to *God's Trombones* why he uses this method rather than the mode of the dialect. The latter would be open to grave abuse in the hands of the unskilled, and the poet writes for all mankind, both learned and unlearned; furthermore, these "black and unknown bards" themselves used the King James Version of the Bible as the best of Elizabethan English, and were quite at home with a version of the Scriptures that meant everything to their moral and religious guidance. They literally memorized whole chapters and books of the Bible; no wonder they excelled in their transmission of its story and its message. When they did add their comments upon the Biblical story, they did so with taste and skill. These have been reverently and faithfully preserved for us by the genius and insight of our poet.

Let me take just three of the greatest of these poem-sermons as types of their message and revelations of the character of the messenger. For imaginative power, "The Creation"; for dramatic intensity, "The Prodigal Son"; and, because we are gathered here to do honor to one who "being dead yet speaketh," for prophetic understanding, "Go Down, Death."

I

"The Creation" is, I believe, the only one of the collection in *God's Trombones* that appeared in a previous volume, our author's famous and well-chosen anthology of Negro poetry. It is a moving and telling account of the first chapter of Genesis, told with abandon, artlessness, and poetic charm. It does no disparagement at all to Genesis itself to say that just as the unknown Hebrew poets and scribes vied with each other, and their rich and imaginative legacy has come to us in that ancient book, so our unknown Negro bards gave their beautifully

wrought expressions into our poet's keeping, until he enriched
them with the artistry of his soul and transmitted them to us.
"The Creation" has the breadth of tone not unlike that of the
trombone, and it has also the most delicate and subtle nuances
that could ever arrest and hold the finer instincts. From the
boldness of "And God stepped out on space" at the beginning
of this fine poem, to the very closing grandeur of "And man
became a living soul. Amen," one feels the glow of a great
experience, and the cosmic significance of human life in its
relation to God and the world.

One may dare to say that this poem is a rebuke to those of
us prosy and matter-of-fact souls who have to measure and
estimate everything. No one who is lacking in fancy and inven-
tion can ever begin to understand the meaning of this sermon
of the time "when the morning stars sang together, and all the
sons of God shouted for joy." Dull souls will see no beauty in
it; materialistic minds will cavil at its childlike faith and won-
ders; only "the pure in heart," like our gentle and discerning
friend James Weldon Johnson, can see its loveliness, and its
freshness and joy. "The Creation" is a sort of epic of the
universe in miniature; it is like gathering up all the meaning
of life and truth in one scene, but oh, what an exhilarating and
utterly truthful portrayal it is! Not afraid nor ashamed of the
pleasures of the imagination, our poet here leads us into some
of the rarest and happiest secrets of a valid religious experience.
True religion is never skeptical about imagination. It is only
petty souls that fret who find fault with everything that cannot
respond to the five physical senses. Thank God, good poets and
good preachers are able to deliver us from such pettiness!

II

We now turn to that highly dramatic sermon which pays
great tribute to the most famous of the Master's parables in the
New Testament. This is entitled simply and effectively "The
Prodigal Son." Even though the original in Luke 15 is told for
a far different purpose than the portraiture of a willful and

stubborn youth who had to learn by the bitter hardship of losing his money, friends, and reputation, yet so embedded in the popular mind is the feeling that the prodigal is the hero of the tale that we shall always know the story as "The Prodigal Son."

Here the motif is one of the finest realism. And because there is so much false realism in our modern world that cries out for the crude, the ghastly, the ugly, and the brutal in the name of realism, it is all the more to the point that both in Luke 15 and in James Weldon Johnson's conception of it in this powerful and colorful drama-sermon, we have every movement, every human touch, every little petty conceit and every noble impulse alike set down with clarity and with honesty. The prodigal's father is a gentle soul, who is loving and forgiving; he is not a doddering and foolish old parent, trifling with indulgence toward a scoundrel. The prodigal himself is far from a mere scapegrace; he has his moments of intense conviction and inward recognition of a higher destiny than a swine pen in a foreign country. The highly touched coloring in the description of the "far-off country" is more highly than ever achieved in naming it "Babylon" (who but a poet would have thought of that!) where a youth "wasted his substance in riotous living," and where the wine and perfume of his prostitute-friends intoxicated his body and soul. It is superb art, compelling one's genuine admiration, and finally winning one's unbounded enthusiasm for both the father's patient and conquering kindness and the complete turning of the onetime man of the world and "man about town" into a repentant and chastened searcher after a life of truth and goodness. Here is realism if you want it! Let our pioneer preachers and our discerning poet instruct us, if we are wise!

III

But perhaps our poet will be known best of all for the final one of these three which are suggested for the study of types of truth in forms of beauty. This one is known as "Go Down,

Death" and is the story of a humble woman down in Savannah, Georgia, on the Yamacraw River, who is dying. It is really her funeral sermon, and Sister Caroline is being both lamented and eulogized. And here the great meaning is that of a prophetic power which all valid religion has ever held in high esteem. Prophecy, as wise poets and preachers know, is not a magical foretelling of events; it is, rather, an interpretation of all events, so that life becomes predictable, and with full meaning, because of such a power. Our poet is fully aware of this meaning of prophecy, and my only wish, as I read this moving and beautiful poem, "Go Down, Death," is that not only should all poets emulate this understanding but also that all preachers should be compelled to study this poem before they ever preach from the book of Revelation. For the imagery of the poem is taken boldly from that difficult and occult book. Woe betide the souls that take lightly and stupidly such a book for their theme! The life of Sister Caroline, which had such little significance here in this world of sin and sorrow, now, by the act of God himself, takes on eternal and boundless significance. And is this not the genius of all true knowledge and art and religion? Do not these great illuminators of human life tell us that we are more than all else, and that the whole creation is made for our use and our high destiny? And do not such truths make life take new and mighty meaning in the scheme of things? We are here on the high grounds of the poet's pilgrimage. He has taken us with him to the Delectable Mountains of the Soul. From this spiritual plateau we may view life, death, and the great things of God and humanity with understanding, with confidence, and with assurance.

"He being dead yet speaketh."

9
It's Either Up or Down

HENRY BRADFORD, JR.
Second Cumberland Presbyterian Church
Huntsville, Alabama

Henry Bradford, Jr., is one of the clergy who possess triple compe-
tence. He is a successful teacher, an accomplished musician, and a
good preacher.

Bradford was born in New Orleans and graduated from Dillard
University, Oberlin School of Theology, and Columbia University.
He also studied at Juilliard School of Music, Chicago Musical College, New England Conservatory of Music, and Oberlin Conservatory of Music. Alabama A & M University has called him to serve
as chairperson of the Department of Music and as university chaplain.

He has served on various boards of many community organizations.
He is the recipient of several citations and awards.

Henry Bradford is president of the Board of Education and Publi-
cations and chairperson of the National Centennial Committee of
the Cumberland Presbyterian Church. He is recognized as one of the
efficient and effective leaders of his denomination.

The sermon entitled "It's Either Up or Down" was delivered at
the Second Cumberland Presbyterian Church, Huntsville, Alabama,
on Sunday, January 11, 1976. This sermon challenged the congregants, especially young people, to worship sincerely and think deeply
regarding their Christian commitment.

SERMON 9

Who shall ascend into the hill of the Lord?

PSALM 24:3

The Bible embraces the concept that life is either an ascent experience or a descent experience. People go either up or down in their spiritual enrichment and development; and these are the only real alternatives open to them.

In Psalm 24 the question comes: "Who shall ascend into the hill of the Lord?" Even here, the suggestion is that life is not level. Life is a slope. Life is not flat, it is an incline.

Not long ago I had the privilege of visiting Chattanooga, Tennessee. Outside that city, there is a vehicle that ascends and descends Lookout Mountain. It's called "The Incline." It provided an exciting experience for me as the children and I went up the slope of that mountain, slowly but surely. The speed was as it was because of the slant grade that the car had to overcome. It kept moving, upward and onward, until at last it reached the summit of that mountain. And after a brief respite for the passengers to embark, it was down again, only to continue the same process until closing time. As I pondered that sight I soliloquized: "Life is like that! It's either up or down." It's not an enjoyable, serene, verdant meadow; life is a hillside—yes, a mountain. As we live, we go either one way or the other.

One poet put it beautifully. He said:

> To every man there openeth
> A Way, and Ways, and a Way,
> And the High Soul climbs the High way,
> And the Low Soul gropes the Low,
> And in between, on the misty flats,
> The rest drift to and fro.
> But to every man there openeth
> A High Way, and a Low.
> And every man decideth
> The Way his soul shall go.
>
> —*John Oxenham*

I

The quality of our life is determined by the direction in which we look. We are measured by our intention; tested by our ambition; evaluated by our desire and not always by our achievement. The set of the sail is what really tests people. This is what really separates people as our Lord said he would. He said, "When the Son of man shall come in his glory, and all the holy angels with him, then shall he sit upon the throne of his glory: And before him shall be gathered all nations: and he shall separate them one from another, as a shepherd divideth his sheep from goats: And he shall set the sheep on his right hand, but the goats on the left" (Matt. 25:31–33). Scholars relate that in Palestine the sheep were white and the goats were black. Here we go again! The worst of everything is equated with blackness; but that has but little to do with quality. I would imagine there are some *beautiful* black goats as there are beautiful *white* sheep. The same is true of human beings. What is important is not color really but whether there's quality; and quality can be determined by the direction of our vision. It's greatly important whether your face is set toward the summit or the base of the hill.

Psychologists have proved long since that people of merit can come from either the east side or the west side of the tracks. They have discovered that poor folks can have high intelligence quotients as well as affluent ones. The difference might be in the degree of cultural exposure. The decisive thing in all of this is how that *potential* will be utilized.

A black dope pusher might have an excellent IQ, but if he uses it to stealthily inveigle young blacks like those in your neighborhood, young blacks like those in your family, to face a direction that brings only the base of the hill into focus, then he's not using his potential wisely and the victim becomes so because he has failed to use his.

A policeman can have superior potential and an enviable degree of professional skill. However, if that skill is fused with his racial prejudice which leads him to impose an extraordinary measure of brutality on anything with black skin, the view of that officer is directed toward the wrong part of the hill. His victims are often influenced to lower their view too.

Someone has said that how a warrior falls in battle provides a valid index to his heroism or his cowardice. Surely if the fatal wounds appear in the back of his body, the conclusion well might be that he was a coward. If the fatal wounds appear in the chest or stomach area, the verdict would be that he probably was facing forward. Hence, a hero had fallen! It's the direction in which we look—up or down—that decides the quality of our character, the depth of our commitment, and the worth of our loyalty to our Lord and Savior, Jesus Christ. That's why the Holy Bible placed so much stress upon the *look*. It says, *"Look* unto me and be saved."

"I will *lift up my eyes* unto the hills" (Ps. 121:1). We are saved from our lower selves, we are saved from shallowness, by looking upward.

The apostle Paul said that always we must be "looking unto Jesus the author and finisher of our faith" (Heb. 12:2).

The person who looks unto God is a saved man because *that* look means he's a climber and a struggler. It means that his face is on things above, where Christ Jesus sits on the right hand of God. Indeed, our look is an indication of our dedication.

My grandmother was much like your grandmother. In my

mind's eye I can see her now with long apron, hanging up clothes on the line in the backyard of her home where the ground had no grass and had been *purposely* made smooth like an onion, as she sang:

> Climbin' up the mountain, chillun;
> Didn't come here fo' to stay.
> If I never more see you again,
> I'll meet you at the Judgment Day.

It's not easy for black folks in America to look up all the time, but the redeemed ones are known by whether we're looking *up* or *down!*

II

There's a second thing which this text suggests. This second fact is that it's impossible to stand still. Life would be one monotonous encounter if we went on day after day, month after month, year after year, on the same level. Life is not level! It's as a hillside! I think you ought to say "A-men" to that!

The moment we cease to climb, we slide back. We either get better, my friends, or we get worse. Yes, you can't rest on past laurels. If you attempt to do that, nobody can see them, because you're resting on them. We've got to "keep on truckin'" as time marches on.

Jesse Owens could never have won the coveted gold medal he won years ago at the Olympics in Germany if he had been satisfied merely with the races he had won elsewhere prior to that eventful experience. He had to keep practicing, keep timing himself, keep pushing. He had several strikes against him in Germany. For one thing, Adolf Hitler had told his home folks that blacks had tails. Their blatant ignorance led them to fix their vision where tails usually extend. They saw nothing but "a fine brown frame" moving like lightning!

Charles Drew never could have discovered the blood plasma process if he had stopped seeking and searching and if he had succumbed to the incalculable racial odds confronting him. As

God would have it, he kept on moving. He refused to stand
still. Unfortunately he died on an Alabama highway by bleeding to death, because the ambulance that was on the scene
refused to transport him to the hospital from which it was
dispatched because he was black. When the ambulance for
black citizens eventually reached the site of the accident, it was
too late. He died from the lack of that which he discovered to
help save the lives of so many others.

No! No! You cannot be satisfied with *what* you are now, nor
with *where* you are now. That's stagnation, and a stagnant life
is an ineffective life. No black person in America today can be
satisfied, neither economically, nor academically, nor politically, nor morally, nor spiritually!

Innumerable portals are now open to black folks in this
country. One of these is the freedom to register and vote.
However, even in this day of newfound opportunities, there are
still thousands and thousands of blacks who are not registered
voters, both in the North and in the South. Voting rights have
caused many positive things to happen, but many more could
occur if the voting pressure were applied more comprehen-
sively. We must go up!

It is possible to go to schools that were heretofore closed to
the enrollment of blacks, yet there are too many dropouts.
Blacks have got to encourage each other and assist each other
in the matter of staying in school. Preparation is the key that
will yet unlock many more doors. That preparation cannot be
obtained by giving up at the base of the hill. It must be the
top or nothing, and one has to struggle, strain, and sacrifice to
get there. Nothing less will do! Often, defeat is due to the
misplacement of values. It's not the fast car, the sharp suit, the
loud mouth, the latest handshake, that matters. Real worth is
often inherent in *no* car, the *neat* suit, the modulated voice
which is gifted with a good command of "the mother tongue"
and a handshake that says, "I have confidence in myself, in
God, and in what I can do! I am mentally awake and morally
straight."

The Pharisee in the Temple had hit a plateau. He thanked God that he was not as other men, and that was it. He was satisfied with his achievement and was thereafter complacent.

The rich young ruler went away sorrowful but he was satisfied even in his sorrow.

Felix, the great Jewish leader, was satisfied in his spiritual stagnation. He told the apostle to come back to talk when he had more time to confer. Paul left him basking in his spiritual petrification.

What all these brothers did not know was that it's impossible to stand still.

The African slaves who became American Christians could have been satisfied and quit serving the Lord Jesus Christ. Instead, they made beautiful "noise" that was heard all over the nation! They sang:

> Oh, freedom! Oh, freedom!
> Before I'd be a slave,
> I'd be buried in my grave;
> And go home to my Lord and be free!

The youth of black America could have remained satisfied in the '50s and the '60s.

Martin Luther King could have remained satisfied in his time. Instead, he led in the social transformation of America. I'm different and you're different because he ascended into the hill of the Lord.

The good things of earth, the best things in life, the superior award of heaven, are all on high! To get there, we must climb the hill; and climbing is not easy.

Every time we're admonished to be holy, to render service, we're told to apply a bit more effort lest we stand still. That's why Jesus said, *"Strive* to enter in at the strait gate." You can't remain constant, nor satisfied.

I'm trampin', trampin',
Trying to make heaven my home.
I'm trampin', trampin',
Trying to make heaven my home.

It's a steady climb to heaven;
Isaac Watts, an extraordinary soldier of the cross, put it into words which are in almost every hymnal.

Must I be carried to the skies
On flowery beds of ease,
While others fought to win the prize
And sailed through bloody seas?

Sure, I must fight if I would reign;
Increase my courage, Lord!
I'll bear the toil, endure the pain,
Supported by thy Word.

Who shall ascend into the hill of the Lord, and who shall stand in his holy place?
What is your answer?

10
The Glory of the Temple

EUGENE S. CALLENDER
Church of the Master
New York, New York

Eugene Callender's call to preach refused to take leave of him. His excursion into work as a member of the Urban League's staff did not silence it. Neither did his stint with the Housing Department and the New York Urban Coalition or his co-hosting of a popular television program cause it to beat a retreat. It persisted so forceably until in 1976 he returned to full-time service as preacher and pastor of the Church of the Master, where he formerly served as associate pastor.

The sermon "The Glory of the Temple" was delivered in the Church of the Master during the occasion of the dedication of the new sanctuary. In it, this Boston native lifts the rich symbolism of the Jewish Temple out of its traditional context and places it in the black milieu. He also sprinkles it with significant clues regarding worship in the black experience.

Eugene Callender is one of the Presbyterian preachers who has not allowed membership in a white church to divorce him from the black idiom. He continues to demonstrate how ebony messengers can keep the black preaching tradition alive in white denominations.

SERMON 10

For a day in thy courts is better than a thousand elsewhere. I would rather
be a doorkeeper in the house of my God than dwell in the tents of wickedness.

PSALM 84:10

In their desire to make the Infinite intelligible and express-
ible, the Hebrews used symbolism. They used material objects
to represent the divine. They made great use of symbols, not
as objects of worship, but as aids to worship. They made an ark;
they built a tabernacle for the wilderness journeys. They made
cherubim and seraphim to represent God's angels, or messengers. They built an altar as a place of sacrifice, but their greatest
and most significant attempt to reveal to men the presence of
God was the holy Temple. For the Temple was regarded as
divinity's dwelling place.

The erection of temples is not peculiar to the Judeo-Chris-
tian tradition. Other peoples—Babylonians, Persians, Greeks,
and Romans—have built out of rock and clay sanctuaries for
their deities. Many of the world's greatest architectural feats
are represented in temples of worship built to the glory of both
mythological gods and the one true God.

In Hebrew thought, the Temple embodied every vital aspect
of their religion. The divine presence abode there in the daz-
zling "glory cloud" which settled down over the Holy of Holies.
The Ark of the Covenant rested in the inner chamber, symbol-
izing God's meeting with his people on the ground of atone-
ment. They did not think that God was confined to the Temple or to any earthly structure. They simply felt that the
Temple was their special meeting place. No people in the long

run of human history have been more ardent in, and devoted to, "temple worship." Their favorite name for this place was "the house of the Lord." Listen to their ecstatic utterances:

> Surely goodness and mercy shall follow me all the
> days of my life:
> And I will dwell in the house of the Lord for ever.
> (Ps. 23:6)

> One thing have I desired of the Lord, that will I
> seek after;
> That I may dwell in the house of the Lord all the
> days of my life,
> To behold the beauty of the Lord, and to inquire in
> his temple.
> (Ps. 27:4)

> I was glad when they said unto me,
> Let us go into the house of the Lord.
> (Ps. 122:1)

And in the 84th Psalm, the psalm that Fleming James has called "the supreme psalm of the sanctuary," the sons of Korah, the temple singers, sang:

> How amiable are thy tabernacles, O Lord of hosts!
> My soul longeth, yea, even fainteth for the
> courts of the Lord. . . .
> For a day in thy courts is better than a thousand.
> I had rather be a doorkeeper in the house of my God,
> Than to dwell in the tents of wickedness.
> (Ps. 84:1–2, 10)

They talked about, they sang about, and they thanked God for—"the glory of the temple."

What is the modern attitude toward the temple? How do we regard the house of the Lord? Do contemporary Christians have the kind of fervor that makes them say, "The zeal of thine house hath eaten me up"? Do we attach sacred significance to temples of worship? Is there any holy ground left? One is almost led to say, "No!" Almost nothing is regarded as sacred anymore. It is highly important how we regard "the house of the Lord." Since the dawning of the Gospel Day, Christians have attached infinite worth to the temple. In early times they found it necessary to meet from house to house, but even then a humble abode was made the dwelling place of the Godhead. So the question has relevance—what is our attitude toward the temple?

Every physical structure symbolizes something. The schoolhouse symbolizes man's quest for knowledge; the business building symbolizes commerce and trade. What does the temple symbolize? Does it still represent the place of divine confrontation? Do we still prefer it above our chief joy?

Upon examination, we find there is widespread decline in temple enthusiasm, particularly within the inner city. This is revealed in the death of so many inner-city churches. Within a five-year period the population increased by 200,000 in an area of lower Manhattan, and during the same period 17 churches went out of existence. This is the pattern in large cities across the nation. But aside from this phenomenon, there is a general decline in enthusiasm for God's house. What is to blame? What are the contributing factors? There are at least three things that have contributed to the decline.

In the first place, our time is marked by a loss of the sense of awe and mystery. We are no longer thrilled by nature's marvels. We can soar higher than the eagle, we can swim as deep as the whale, but we are no longer charmed by the singing of a bird and the antics of a squirrel. Most of us in this land are urban dwellers, and in the city rain is more of a nuisance than a blessing. Snow immobilizes and slows us down. The sound of a thunderclap is a bad omen. The starry heavens do not speak to our hearts. We no longer look for the rainbow after the storm. The buzz of a bee and the chirp of a cricket stir no emotions. In short, we are dehumanized. And whenever the creation, with all its awe and wonder, fails to churn our emotions, we lose our awareness of the Creator behind all creation. Hence, the temple of God becomes a mausoleum for dead liturgies, dead rituals, and dead traditions. We are now awestricken by the products of Hollywood and the scientific laboratory. We do not concern ourselves with what God is doing. We are concerned about what science will do next. Science is our shepherd and we need not pray. The cynic passes by the temple and says as he makes his way, "Nothing happens here."

A second reason for the loss of temple enthusiasm is the irrelevancy of much contemporary preaching. Much of today's preaching falls into one of two categories, either a narrow orthodoxy or a broad liberalism, and both are wrong! Narrow orthodoxy is concerned only with personal salvation; broad liberalism is concerned only with social salvation. Both miss the mark because the great Head of the church is concerned with both. God desires our personal salvation, but he does not want our light hidden under a bushel. God desires that social structures be transformed, but he does not want us to ignore the need for men to be delivered from their sins. "Faith without works is dead," and works without faith are likewise dead. The church has only one mission—the proclamation of the gospel —but it must relate to the times or it becomes irrelevant and powerless. Whenever preaching becomes irrelevant, the temple ceases to have a purpose for its existence.

A third factor that has dampened man's enthusiasm for the temple is the church's capitulation to the world. The church, in many instances, has become a prisoner of its cultural environment. The church has taken on the glow and character of surrounding secular institutions. There is a tendency to lump the church and other agencies of goodwill together and set them in a common mold. The church should never be forced into a kind of posture where men will say, "The church is no different from other agencies." A dialectical tension must always be maintained between our divine mission and our human function. We are first of all custodians and promulgators of "the faith . . . once delivered unto the saints," and our human function, or work in the world, should always reflect our historic divinity. We should never lose sight of home base. We should never become prisoners of the surrounding culture.

It is tragically true that temple enthusiasm has waned. Modern man has little regard for God's house. Many stand outside and criticize. Few come in and seek its improvement. But I submit to you the belief of my heart, soul, and mind that the temple, in its weakness and in its strength, at its worst and at its best, has a particular glory paralleled by no other place. It is shunned by many, scorned by a host, and even despised by some. But its glory is predicated not on what men say about it nor on who enters its gates, but on Whom it represents.

The glory of the temple is to be seen in what happens within its courts. It is the place of encounter between man and his Maker. It is the soul's shaping ground. It is the place where man meets God. It is the most hallowed spot on earth. For in the temple man is first of all brought face to face with God as He is. Listen to Isaiah as he talks about his temple experience: "I saw also the Lord . . . high and lifted up." That is God as He is. In the temple we are also brought face to face with man as he is: "Woe is me! for I am undone; because I am a man of unclean lips, and I dwell in the midst of a people of unclean lips." That is man as he is. In the temple we are, moreover, brought face to face with what man can become: "Then flew one of the seraphim unto me, having a live coal in his hand, which he had taken with the tongs from off the altar: and he laid it upon my mouth, and said, Lo, this hath touched thy lips; and thine iniquity is taken away." Here we touch the garment of the living God. It is no wonder then that the psalmist declared: "A day in thy courts is better than a thousand elsewhere. I would rather be a doorkeeper in the house of my God than dwell in the tents of wickedness."

The glory of the Temple is also seen in its open invitation to all men. It is the "house of prayer for all nations." There is "plenty good room" for all of God's children. The Lord of the temple bids all to come and drink freely from the wells of salvation. All men are included in the blessed invitation, "Whosoever will, let him come." It is painfully true that man in his sinful pride has built temples of worship for certain people only. Congregations have been established and temples built along class and racial lines, but wherever God's Spirit truly dwells, the temple gates swing open to all men. Wherever the Lord is loved, the rich and the poor, the high and the low, all meet together. Every human institution has, by and large, segregated and classified people according to certain criteria. Where we live, where we learn, what we wear, and what we eat are determined in the main by the degree of our affluence. It is only within the courts of the Temple of God that the foolish lines that separate men are erased. When men cross the threshold of the sacred place, rank and status disappear. It is the Lord's house. You come not by human invitation but by divine arrangement. Your admittance was secured by a transaction on Calvary. All men must humble themselves in the presence of God, and I'm glad that's the way it is. This is the house of God for all people. The Ph.D. is welcome, the washwoman is welcome, and both of them can sit together and feel at home. There is room enough, and God is big enough for every genuine emotion to be expressed in this place. The intellectual, the mystic, the weeper, and the "shouter" are all welcome, and whatever they do that is genuine and sincere is all right with God and should be all right with us all. Sit in calm meditation if you choose, contemplate the greatness of God if you desire. Cry if you must. Shout if you can't help it. Only be genuine and sincere in whatever you do.

Well, we live in an age when temple enthusiasm has waned. Many do not delight in God's house, but thanks be to God some still sing the psalmist's song. Why are you yet here? You are here because of deep devotion. You've been gripped by God's Spirit. You've been touched by his love. You've been redeemed by his grace. That's the answer! God has you in his embrace. You met him one day in one of his temples. It may have been in a little frame church in a rural setting, or it may have been in a city temple. But you met him one day! It may have been in a place where an old gray-haired preacher presided, or it may have been in a place where a young preacher held forth. But you met him one day! It may have been where they sang without accompaniment, or it may have been where the organ was used. But you met him one day! You may have been young and undefiled, or you may have been old and wretched. But you met him one day! You went to God's house. You heard the man of God preach the Word. You saw God as he is. You saw yourself as you were. You saw what, by the grace of God, you could become. You believed and you repented. You met God one day in a temple somewhere and you can never forget the place.

Every now and then I take a walk along memory lane and think of that sacred place where I first met the Lord. As a lad, my father took me by the hand and led me to the temple. He told me it was God's house. He taught me to love, honor, and respect it. Years have passed; I now have children of my own and I am telling them the same thing. There is no place like it. I prefer it above my chief joys. I met God in the temple. I was baptized in the temple. I grew up in the temple. I now serve in the temple. I still meet God in the temple. And one day when the clouded skyline of my own mortality fades into oblivion in response to the invariable fact of death, I shall take my flight to the Holy City, where no temple is needed. But until that day,

> a day in thy courts is better than a thousand elsewhere. I would rather be a doorkeeper in the house of my God than dwell in the tents of wickedness.

11

The Patience to Wait

KATIE G. CANNON
Church of the Ascension
New York, New York

Katie Cannon was the first black woman ordained to preach in The United Presbyterian Church in the United States of America. This accomplishment has inspired and challenged some of her black sisters to complete their seminary training and apply for ordination.

The Rev. Katie Cannon was born in Kannapolis, North Carolina. Her undergraduate study was done at Johnson C. Smith University, and she graduated from Johnson C. Smith Theological Seminary. She is presently a doctoral candidate at Union Theological Seminary in New York City.

Cannon has refused to alienate herself from idiomatic expressions. She has proudly brought them from Kannapolis to New York City. In fact, she takes them into many of the pulpits where she preaches. Some evidence of this fact is found in the sermon "The Patience to Wait." This sermon was delivered in the Presbyterian Church of the Ascension in New York City.

Katie Cannon has served as a chaplain intern at the Georgia Retardation Center and as assistant at the Church of the Master. She is interim pastor in the Church of the Ascension.

SERMON 11

And Esau said to Jacob, Feed me, I pray thee, with that same red pottage; for I am faint: therefore was his name called Edom.

GENESIS 25:30

Our meditation on this special Sunday is taken from the book of Genesis, chapter 25, verses 29 through 34, wherein Isaac has taken Rebekah to be his lawful and wedded wife. Now, this couple could not have children, due to medical or psychological complications. There was nothing wrong with them physically, but still they had not given birth to a child, which I am sure gave them a great deal of concern as it would most married couples. Eventually, after concentrated effort, the couple was blessed with a set of twin sons who were named Esau and Jacob.

As Esau and Jacob grew, they represented two distinct individuals. Esau was the outstanding, outgoing, athletic kind of person—husky, hairy, broad-chested, and always trying to prove himself physically. Jacob was the quiet, thinking, intellectual kind of person—clever, scheming, conniving, and always figuring how to beat somebody out of something.

However, Esau had one advantage over Jacob—namely, that he was the first of the twins to come out at birth, meaning that he was supposed to enjoy the rights and privileges of the family inheritance according to the Hebrew custom. But Esau was not the most clever person in the world—even though he could "chunk" a rock a mile because of strong, physical muscles. And thus, the schemer actually enjoyed the rights and privileges of the family inheritance eventually, because he could outfox with

84

sly, slick ways this nonthinking brute of a brother. So, let us see how the schemer outfoxed the athlete, as our text indicates in a modern-day paraphrased expression.

The paraphrased expression says this: Once when Jacob was boiling pottage, that is, possibly warming "lentils and *rice*," Esau came in from the field famished, that is, real, real "hongry." And Esau begged Jacob, saying "Let me eat some of that pottage, for I am famished." And Jacob, the perennial schemer, said, "First, give me your birthright." In other words, "Go find daddy's insurance policy and sign it over to me." Esau said, "I am about to die from hunger; of what use is a birthright to me, a person who needs physical strength?" After Esau came back with the insurance policy, Jacob said, "Swear to me first." That is, "Hold up your right hand 'fore' God and 'clare' to me that you will never come back for this insurance policy." So Esau swore to him; he held up his right hand "fore" God that he would never come back after it, and sold his birthright to Jacob. Then Jacob gave Esau the bread and pottage of lentils, and something to drink. Esau ate and drank all that was set before him and rose and went away from the table. Thus, Esau despised his birthright, that is, he considered this insurance policy which required his waiting for a period of time to be of less value than the peas and rice there before him.

The subject that I have chosen to speak to you about this morning is "The Patience to Wait."

In the day-to-day hustle and bustle of these inflationary times we wake up and discover a haunting contradiction in our being—that is, we find ourselves from time to time being both Esau and Jacob. We find ourselves both loving yet hating, forgiving yet resentful, committed yet indecisive, seeing the future yet blind to it, conservative yet radical, thinking high and noble thoughts yet lowdown and nasty thoughts—simply because we do not have the patience to wait on the Lord.

Our concern this morning is how we mess ourselves up in those things which cannot come into being at the present time, due to our failure to maintain patience. Like Esau, we come to the point of saying, "I'll die if I don't get it now." If we have to wait for it, we find ourselves throwing temper tantrums, having all kinds of "hissy fits" full of many changes. We become men and women who sell our birthright—simply because time is something that gives us a hang-up, especially when it comes to waiting on the Lord for his blessings. Like Esau, we shout continually, *"I'll die if I don't get it now!"*

So, *what* we are saying here is that we often live out our days with our being torn asunder, due to our lack of knowledge about how to maintain our basic loyalty to our God as it relates to waiting upon the Lord for blessings in the future. *We just don't know how to wait for tomorrow's blessings.*

Now, I want to suggest three things we must do which will reflect our patience to wait on the Lord. They will prevent us from selling our birthright.

The first thing that each of us must do in order to never again sell or give away our birthright is that we must *recall* exactly what it is that God gave to us at birth.

By this I mean that the very first thing that each of us must do is bring to the front of our minds the unique and distinct purpose for which God created us. We must remember our beginnings. We must keep fresh in our minds that God created us male and female in God's own image. We must remember that God made us just a little less than the angels. We must revive in our beings testimonies regarding how God brought us forth in a miraculous birth and gave us something that no one else on this earth has so that we can help fulfill his purpose.

In other words, we must recall our birthright by asking ourselves some soul-searching questions, such as: "For what purpose did God create us?" "What is the reason for God's amazing grace which has spared us to live to this day?" "What is our reason for living?" We need to get away from the noisy crowds and search our souls regarding the meaning of our lives.

If we stop and think of all the people who have been murdered on the streets of New York; and if we recall the many lives that have been taken on the war-torn battlefields of the world; if we consider the many brothers and sisters whose essence was snuffed out in accidents or diseases of one kind or another; if we pause and reflect on the hundreds upon hundreds who have been wiped out in tornadoes, earthquakes, fires, famines, floods, and in all kinds of natural disasters, we recognize the need to recall for what distinct purpose God has let us remain to this very day. We must take time out and turn over in our minds exactly what is our God-given birthright. What blessing did God give to us that we must wait for it to mature in the future?

What I am saying, Church, is that we all *do* have the drum major instinct. We hunger to be superstars. We all have burning desires to be somebody, and if we will just bring to the front of our minds the person that God created us to be, then we can receive our blessing of somebodiness from the divine giver of life. None of us has earned the right to be here this morning clothed in our right minds with the blood warm and moving through our veins, but it is because of Almighty God's amazing grace that we have been spared to give to the world what God has given to us. This morning, brothers and sisters, we are not stretched out on our cooling boards of death, because God has seen fit to allow us to participate in life another day, and with this in mind we must recall the purpose for which God has brought us thus far on our way.

We must recall the person whom God created us to be so that we can internally know how we really are and what our living truly means. I firmly believe that we must embrace this first element of recalling our birthright so that we can have the patience to hold on to our God. And as we recall, as we turn over again and again in our minds the unique gifts which God has given to each of us, we become rooted like a tree that is planted by the waters and shall not be moved. For if we recall God's divine purpose for our living, then and only then will we be on our way to rid ourselves of hang-ups with time. We will be able to stop messing ourselves up in grabbing hastily to satisfy our passing hunger pains. We will be able to hold on to God's unchanging hand.

Now, the second thing that each of us must do in order not to sell or give away our birthright is that we must replan our

lives so that we can have the patience to wait on the Lord for
his blessings. In other words, once we have recalled the purpose
for which God created us, then the next step is to carry that
purpose out in our daily living. This second alternative is calling
for us to devise new patterns of living. We must reshape our
lives. We must map out and plot our course of action in a new
light of obedience to God and to each other. What this boils
down to is that we have to walk a new walk and talk a new talk.

For most of us this is very difficult because we have swapped
our gold for sand so often that we probably don't know which
is which. Thus, when we recalled our purpose for living, when
we brought forth in our minds our God-given birthright, a
number of us found that we clamor for leadership all the time,
and we choose our friends, marriage partners, jobs, neighbor-
hoods, and churches just so we can make a favorable impression
on people around us.

Now, what this means is that when we "recalled" our birthright some of us found that many times we have been modern-
day Esaus who need to reshape our living. Some of us may have
found that we sold our birthright to our mothers, our fathers,
our brothers, our sisters, our children, or to our grandchildren.
Others of us may have found that we gave our God-given rights
to our husbands, wives, or to the material gains of this world.
And whether we are now in positions that we obtained honestly
or dishonestly, or whether we are in relationships that we
manipulated and used people so that others would think highly
of us, most of us cannot go back and undo what is already done.
But we can begin to reshape our living with new alternatives
for being the true person that God created us to be. Once we
have an understanding of our God-given purpose in life, then
we are ready to act accordingly.

For instance, some of us may realize that to reshape our living according to the will of God we must make an about-face.
Some of us have to make some serious and drastic changes in that
we may have to change our marriage partners, select new friends,
or move to a cheaper neighborhood. Others of us may find that
in order to let our birthright mature we need to go back to school

or finish the schools that we have already started. A few of us may find that as we reshape our living we might have to eliminate some of our partying time, give up some of our prime time for watching television, and decide to work more meaningfully with people in our church and in the community.

Still another group may find that in order to reinstate their birthright they need to give some time to visiting the sick and shut-ins, participating in activities for senior citizens, joining the senior choir, volunteering for membership in Sunday school or the Bible study groups.

Now, the third and final thing that all of us must do in order not to sell or give away our birthright is that we must rededicate ourselves to God so that we can have the patience to wait on the Lord for his blessings.

By this I mean that once we recall our birthright and we begin to reshape our living in that manner, we are ready to be sanctified. When we are sanctified, we must give glory and honor to the one and only God in all that we say and do. To have the patience to wait we must give ourselves over to the Lord and let God mold us and God make us, let God fill us and use us, so that the Spirit of the living God will fall afresh upon us.

This third step is calling for us to turn to the great Jehovah in prayer day by day. We must pray in earnestness and meditate sincerely. In other words, we must not only talk with God, but we must also listen to what God is commanding us to do specifically as we go through each day. The way that we can see the will of God more clearly, the direction that we can follow God more nearly, and the pattern in which we can love each other more dearly is that we have to humble ourselves like empty pitchers before a full fountain. Sisters and brothers, we must touch base in prayer and meditate daily so that our birthright will be forever engrained inside of us. We must rededicate ourselves as often as we can so that we will not backslide into being Esau over and over again. Rededication strengthens us so that we don't have to throw temper tantrums and go through unnecessary changes of selling our souls for the price of so-called luxury. Rededication is what helps us as finite creatures to believe in a God who is infinite and who has the knowledge and the power to grant us the patience to wait. The God that we serve, the Yahweh of "I Am That I Am," can give us the fortitude, endurance, self-control, and the serenity to never again throw our God-given pearls to the swine.

And I strongly believe that this third initiative of rededication is a dire need for all of us who want our blessings to mature. We must let go and let God be the master of our fate and the captain of our souls, so that we can hold on to our birthright that God has given to each of us. God will give us the patience to wait, if we believe.

In closing, I ask each of you: Do you want to receive God's true blessings in life? Do you want to put an end to the chaos and confusion that bubbles on your insides? Will you decide at this moment in history to recall, reshape, rededicate your life to God so that your birthright will come into being in the fullness of time? Will you decide to accept God's blessing of tomorrow? Will you accept God's help in retaining your birthright so that not even the gates of hell can prevail against it? Maybe, just maybe, if you decide today as we open the doors of the church; if you decide to recall, reshape, and rededicate your life to God, then you too can make this pledge:

> A charge to keep I have,
>   A God to glorify,
> A never-dying soul to save,
>   And fit it for the sky.
>
> To serve the present age,
>   My calling to fulfill;
> O may it all my powers engage
>   To do my Master's will!
>
> Help me to watch and pray,
>   And on thyself rely,
> And let me ne'er my trust betray,
>   But press to realms on high.
>
>   —*Charles Wesley*

12
On Possessing What Is Yours

ABRAHAM H. PRINCE
Ebenezer United Presbyterian Church
Dalzell, South Carolina

Abraham Prince has been an inspiring and challenging black Presbyterian preacher in the Southeast for many generations. During his long years of dedicated service he has brought fresh courage to discouraged pastors and parishioners. And his sermons have given new hope and determination to formerly disillusioned young people.

"On Possessing What Is Yours" is an inspiring and challenging sermon. It was delivered during a meeting of Fairfield-McClelland Presbytery. In it the preacher issues a clear and discomforting call for ecclesiastical self-development and strength.

Prince was born in Sumter County, South Carolina. He is a graduate of the college and seminary of Biddle (Johnson C. Smith) University.

He was pastor of the Brooklyn Presbyterian Church in Charlotte, North Carolina. He is presently serving Ebenezer United Presbyterian Church, Dalzell, South Carolina.

Abraham Prince has also served the national church as Joint Field Representative of the Boards of Christian Education and National Missions, and as Director of Evangelism for the Synods of the Atlantic and Catawba. The years have not robbed this elder church statesman of his evangelistic zeal and passion for the church. The reader of "On Possessing What Is Yours" will inevitably experience confrontation with each of these forces.

SERMON 12

And Caleb stilled the people before Moses, and said, Let us go up at once, and possess it; for we are well able to overcome it.

NUMBERS 13:30

Imagine a people perplexed and disturbed. See them as they journeyed under the leadership of Moses to a land where they would find solutions for the complexities of their lives. God, who chose Moses, assured him that He would be with him and would help him. God told Moses: "Choose twelve men from the twelve tribes of Israel, and have them go and investigate the land. Command them to observe the people and the general conditions of all things that they would have to live with." They went, in obedience, and investigated the land, the people, and all conditions which they assumed they would have to live with.

They declared it was a goodly land; but, so far as living there, they concluded they could not because the men were great in stature and they were as grasshoppers in the sight of the strangers. They could not conquer the people and the land. Therefore, when the report ended, the listeners were in an uproar. Caleb calmed the people as he said: "Let us go up at once, and possess it; for we are well able to conquer it." The majority had made its report. Caleb made a minority report with emphasis upon the belief that the land could be possessed. Caleb was recognized. His report claimed attention because it focused upon qualities that every great leader must have if he or she would succeed.

Caleb possessed initiative. "Act now and you will overcome the complexities which are evident. See some of the fruits of this land. We only can carry the grapes suspended between two of us. See the tall and big people. Observe that the Sons of Anak dwell here, and in comparison we are as grasshoppers in their sight." The spies minimize themselves and "vaunt" the fact that they could not measure up to the challenges of this land. Caleb saw evidence of their inferiority complex and said: "Rise up immediately! Let us go up, conquer, and possess the land. For we are able to do this."

The initiative exercised by Caleb gives us to understand that if we cease to act and procrastinate when we are face to face with intricate situations, we cannot win. Let's go *now*, for our God dwells in an eternal Now, as there is neither past nor future with him. He is the One who enables us to conquer in his eternal Now. There is nothing to be gained in waiting. Why wait when something can be done now? Let's rise up in God's eternal NOW to trudge heavenward and claim our possession. The effort that we put forth now will enable us to go higher and attain the heights beyond ourselves.

We think now of our mission enterprise both at home and abroad. What fine opportunities we have to seize and use them as stepping-stones to produce and to achieve respect and become more responsible. Dr. Russell Conwell in his book *Acres of Diamonds* cites a man who sold his land because it did not yield. The one who bought it discovered that he had purchased diamonds. The home mission fields where our churches are located are studded with diamonds. But we do not make the yields. So we sell out, desiring a more lucrative field where we feel we can produce more, only to find that we have left diamonds to be discovered by others.

The harder the field, the more it is a test of our ability to prove what is in us. And we can truly fulfill the mission if we act now in the name of God and in his wisdom.

Caleb had not only initiative but a compelling urge. He had faith and determination to possess the promised land. We must possess faith in order to come into possession of the things that we must have to make our ministry effective. Judging from the report of the spies, the people could not see how they could compete with their opponents. They had little faith in themselves and God. Therefore they were unable to cope and compete.

Our mission churches believe that because they are small and seemingly insignificant, big churches are responsible for them. Yet one of the most useful things in our small mission fields is for someone or some force to cause them to know their potential. A cluster of small churches can carry out a project that will affect the lives of many, and will perform the type of service that will eventually enable the small churches to discover that they have the potentialities to become a force for good. Also, they will realize that it is not the size but the contributions that can cause the small churches to be indispensable.

Our home mission fields must produce more administrators who will support others rather than who will rejoice in making others feel that their churches must always be recipients. We will not possess our rightful place until our churches become self-supporting and administer resources to others who are striving to become self-supporting. We would be on our way to independence when we begin to share with others that which we ourselves once rejoiced greatly in. Then we are grown. As long as we feel satisfied in receiving rather than in giving we know that we have not arrived into the promised land.

The response of Caleb has in it a note of strength and respectability. We can possess the promised land because we are able to conquer it. If we truly arrive in this land, there are things we have to conquer. One of them is self.

Alexander the Great conquered the whole world and sat down and wept because he had no more empires to conquer. He found later that he had not conquered himself. We cannot demand respect until we ourselves are respectable. We cannot demand respect if we are forever on the receiving end. We must switch over and become administrators. We must become self-supporting so we can help others who need help. If we are receiving always, we will have nothing to help others with.

Make me a captive, Lord, And then I shall be free;
Force me to render up my sword, And I shall conqueror be.

"Then I can administrate and not receive only."

Caleb declared that the people were able. We say that we are able to do whatever we want to do. Paul declared that he could do all things through Christ, who walks with him. *Is there anything we cannot do for God?* The answer is "No." We can inherit the land. We are able. And this United Presbyterian Church to which we belong may come into possession of all the promises given by God.

As you and I travel life's highway, we pause long enough to hear the voices that declare, "It is impossible." "It is impossible!" The world tells us, "It cannot be done." God says, "It can be done." We need a more radiant life today as we travel toward this land. Footsore and weary, we march on. We camp long enough to hear echoes bid us, "Come higher." Sometimes tired, sometimes disgusted, sometimes wanting to turn back; but then comes a vision of angels camping round and about us to revive our spirit.

Let this presbytery go on to higher heights. Tread all the powers of darkness down! Walk in the light as He is the light. Dream of the land of pure delight. Cease not until you reach the land of self-respect and responsibility where all the faithful are.

God, help this presbytery to strive and come into possession of its rightful place. God, help this presbytery to encourage men and women who, like Caleb, will dare to stand alone and tell the world what can be done. Men and women who will insist that we rise up *now* and move toward making ourselves more respectable and responsible.

The church needs strong men and women to carry out her aims and objectives. She needs men and women of vision who live above the fog of time, men and women who are not afraid to be Calebs and declare that we must go forward to inherit all the things promised us by God.

We have more than two thousand members in this presbytery. The majority will tell you what they cannot do. But now
we need to turn our attention to what we can do in mission,
self-support, and community action. We need to share our
resources and ourselves. We need to reassess our powers and
potentialities, and then say, "We are fully able to possess a
higher place of respectability and responsibility."

The time is not tomorrow, for there may not be a tomorrow.
The time is *now*. Possess what is yours!

13
Is Anybody Listening?

PAUL MARTIN
Redeemer Presbyterian Church
Los Angeles, California

Paul Martin was born in California. Most of his educational preparation was done in the West. All of his professional work has been done in the "Golden Gate State." He is currently serving as pastor of the Redeemer Presbyterian Church in Los Angeles.

These facts, however, should not be interpreted as suggesting that Martin's view of his, or the church's, ministry is parochial or provincial. His interest in the liberation of all oppressed people is genuine, as his contributions to the work of the Committee on the Theology of Liberation and Renewal in the United Presbyterian Church will testify.

The recurring emphasis of Paul Martin's ministry has been to those to whom society refuses to listen, and to those who have been summarily dismissed because they are "lost." This young pastor believes that "there needs to be a concerted effort of the denomination to deal with the lost people of our society who are not only alienated from the church but also from themselves and others."

"Is Anybody Listening?" reveals how this pastor's sermons are consonant with his convictions regarding the church's ministry to the youth. These beliefs have also motivated Martin to give a large measure of his time to service on the following boards of directors: Teen Post, Incorporated, Consumers Advisory Committee, Compton Welfare Planning Council, and the Los Angeles Council of Churches.

SERMON 13

And I heard a great voice out of heaven saying, Behold, the tabernacle of God is with men, and he will dwell with them, and they shall be his people, and God himself shall be with them, and be their God.

REVELATION 21:3

One of the most pressing needs confronting the church today is the need to plan for the challenges that the youth culture presents to the Christian community within the black church.

Dennis Benson, writing in a recent issue of *A.D.* magazine, says: "A young person is in the process of becoming, and today there is no place to become."

In the light of all that we hear and read about our youth today, the suggestion has been made that young people haven't changed much. Our youth are still concerned about many of the same things that were concerns of the generation before them. What has changed, however, is the language that is used by youth of today to demonstrate their concerns and their needs.

In the same issue of *A.D.*, there is the suggestion that our youth fear many of the same kinds of things that we fear as youth. For instance, the writer states that youth are still raising the following questions:

What do I want from life and to do with my life?

Who am I really in this mixed-up world?

How do I decide what is right or wrong in my life?

Whom can I trust with the concerns of my life?

Is there a God or some other presence from whom I can receive direction in my life?

Who is responsible for the shaping of my life? Is it my peer group, my parents, my church, or my environment?

How can I get along better with my parents and the people around me?

How can I be liked and accepted by others and how can I cope with the loneliness and alienation that I feel in the society?

All these questions have been raised as life-shaping questions by every generation. We asked them because we were concerned about the process of maturity—a process that suddenly came upon us, thrusting us into manhood and womanhood from the uncertain years of adolescence. The problem before us is both manifold and complex. It can best be described in the language of our topic—"Is Anybody Listening?"—and in the futuristic tones of the marvelous twenty-first chapter of the book of Revelation. The problem is intensified because the church has taken to heart in times past and in the present the adage: "Youth are to be seen and not heard."

It seems that we who are members of the older society have been guilty of turning the channel, changing the station, or substituting the frequency when our youth have tried to communicate their concerns to us and share their urgent needs with us. This may be one of the reasons why the United Presbyterian witness is not being felt significantly among black youth today. Our communities are full of youth who are seeking a forum from which they can emote. They are hurting for someone to listen, anybody to listen and to respond. The tragedy of the black experience in the community is that we have turned a deaf ear to our youth. We tune them out in home, in school, and in church. We need only remember the cries of our youth during the turbulent '60s which gave birth to efforts to be heard through the educational institutions of our society. This cry was heard on the pathways of the Southern States where our youth led the fight against discrimination and segregation as a testimony to their desire to be heard in the black community of our societies. One cannot doubt that the rise of gangs in the black community is a desire on the part of youth who have been denied a forum the chance to gain a hearing and to be heard. The cry for a new morality among the youthful generation may indeed be the effect of the denial of our society to give youth their proper recognition in the communities of our nation.

I often ask myself:

Is anybody listening?

When youth say, "It isn't the church that turns us off, it's the preachers."

Is anybody listening?

When a young man or woman goes through twelve years of "formal" education in the schools of the black community and graduates without being able to read, write, or interpret an elementary sentence or paragraph.

Is anybody listening?

When youth in the black community spend more money on drugs than they do on candy.

Is anybody listening?

When after spending years of formal training in the educational institutions of the society in preparing for job opportunities just to find that there are no jobs available.

Is anybody listening?

When we as adults—yes, even Christian adults—preach one thing and do another.

Is anybody listening?

When all around us black families and homes are breaking up because of the frustrations that plague the society of our time and day.

Is anybody listening?

When positive images and models of success for our youth no longer exist in our communities; and the only images of success available to them are the pimps, prostitutes, and addicts that stand around on the corners, not to mention the winos that are a part of the scenery of every black community.

Is anybody listening?

When gangs and the breeding grounds for gangs become the dominant pattern for success and recognition for our youth in the black community, and there are no longer any viable alternatives for the youth to "just standing around on the corner and rapping."

Is anybody listening? . . . Is there anybody to listen?

Parents have stopped listening. Schools have stopped listening. Churches have stopped listening. *The church!* God's instrument of salvation. God's new society for the liberation of people. The Servant that Isaiah talked about in the sixty-first chapter as the one who frees from oppression. God's church, the healer of the world's hurt. This great church has also stopped listening and has turned a deaf ear to the cry of youth. How tragic.

Russell Clausen, Youth Secretary of the United Church of Christ, as quoted in the *A.D.* magazine, states: "The Church should be an advocate for all youth in the society, insuring their rights in school and just treatment in the courts."

One has to agree with the intent of Mr. Clausen's statement, but one has to carry it farther than he did. The church *must be the insurer of all rights* of the youth, as it seeks to be the insurer of the rights of all. *Advocate, insurer,* and *justice* —all conditions upon which the Christian church has prided itself since the beginning of its history. The church must spend a great deal of time listening to what the people are saying. This applies to the youth of our culture as well. They, too, long to be heard by the church and for the church to respond to their needs.

It seems right to suggest that the black church ought to be about the task of opening channels that help the youth to be heard in the community; and to be about the urgent business of developing programs that will address the concerns of our youth as they seek to become full participants in the society around them. It further seems right to suggest that the black church establish itself as the forum for youth; and the advocate for the rights of youth who, for whatever reason, are being denied their rights, just as we seek to be an advocate for justice, equality, liberation, and the hungry. It seems right to suggest that in a society comprised of a growing number of youth under the age of twenty-one, when many institutions are turning a deaf ear to youth and their concerns the church ought not to be a part of the process to alienate the youth.

Our world is full of deafening cries going unheard: The cry of welfare mothers on Mother's Day in the black communities; the cry of the lonely and destitute persons who live in the hellholes and alleys of our communities; the cry of the hungry and unclothed, the war-torn refugees. Voices crying in the wilderness for someone, just anyone, to hear their concerns. Our world is full of these ear-piercing cries of hurt ones to which the Christian church in the black community must respond. The black church needs to be on the cutting edge of this concern, helping to clarify, identify, and solve the hurting needs of black youth.

As a participant along with youth in the Christian fellowship, I must endeavor to be patient with the youth and persevere in seeking ways to help youth in church and out of church to reach a solution to those things that bother them. As a black man and a black clergyman, I must be concerned with the plight of the youth in church and community. I must recognize that the youth who need our attention are our youth. They are black and beautiful, like us. They are historically and culturally ours. They are the manifestation of our heritage. They are our future. What we do, we must always do with their best interest at heart. These children are our heirs. Through them our future will or will not be secure. They are all we have. They need our love, our example, our leadership and our commitment. If we fail them, we fail ourselves.

Let me suggest that the black church must desire to be an advocate and a listener to the cry of youth today. The church must begin to plan as hard for youth as it plans for adults. This is a must. We can no longer talk about what we think youth want and need; we must be ready to give them what they ask for. We can no longer allow the sin of complacency to keep us as black church men and women from planning a creative ministry for youth—a ministry that is spiritual and relevant to their concerns. We must again take seriously the magnitude of the Sunday church school as a program to aid spiritually the development of our children and youth—yes, even the adults. We must also find new ways to meet the challenge of this now generation—a generation that wants its reward right now.

This is the challenge that is consummated in the words of the book of Revelation. A word that testifies to the newness of the Christian church and the ability of that same church with the blessings of the Spirit of God to bring about "a new heaven and a new black church for a new black community." As God through Christ guarantees the success of the Christian church, so must we certify the future of our beautiful black youth.

Our youthful generation has been called an "instant-on-culture" and a "want-it-now" generation. As God's black people in his black community, we must be ready to give it to them now.

Is anybody listening? Is there anybody listening?

14
A New Birth of Freedom

CLINTON M. MARSH
Synod of the South
Atlanta, Georgia

Clinton Marsh, whose grandfather was a slave, is the product of
Presbyterian schools that had their beginnings in the new-found
freedom days following the Civil War. Marsh has come a long way
from the red clay roads and white clapboard schoolhouse of Wilcox
County, Alabama, to coveted positions in the United Presbyterian
Church, including that of Moderator of the 185th General Assembly
(1973).

Marsh spent nineteen years in the parish ministry. One year at
Chase City United Presbyterian Church in Chase City, Virginia, and
eighteen action-packed years at the Witherspoon United Presbyterian Church in Indianapolis, Indiana. Here that church, under his
leadership, grew from a struggling congregation of one hundred
members to a strong, vital, witnessing church of over eight hundred
members.

Clinton Marsh served the church overseas in Africa on two unique
assignments. First, as the administrator of the Organizing Assembly
of the All-Africa Conference of Churches, and later, from 1965 to
1969, as the director of the Ecumenical Program for Emergency
Action in Africa.

In 1970 he became "Secretary of Ministries outside the structure
of the Church," in what is now the Synod of Lakes and Prairies. He
played a decisive role in community affairs. In 1974, following a
distinguished year as the Moderator of the 185th General Assembly,
Clinton Marsh was elected to the position of Associate Executive of
the Synod of the South, where he now serves in a sensitive and
effective manner.

"A New Birth of Freedom" is a Bicentennial sermon. It was
prepared and delivered with the intent of motivating listeners to
move beyond the pomp and pageantry of a birthday celebration to
reflect upon America's ministry and mission.

SERMON 14

Behold, I make all things new.

REVELATION 21:5

"Can a man be born when he is old?" queried puzzled Nicodemus. And twentieth-century Nicodemuses echo the question, "What do you mean by 'new birth of freedom'?"

"Yes," replied Jesus to Nicodemus, "but it is a birth of spirit." It is something that happens to the quality of human life as a result of the continuing work of the Creator.

"Yes," echoes God in the book of Revelation. "Behold, I make all things new."

Some think that this new birth can happen only in individual lives. Some think that God's affirmation that he makes all things new relates only to the long hereafter. But the Creator who carefully designed not only humanity but the need for humanity to function in systems of relationships is not indifferent to the quality of man's physical, social, economic, and political environment and to the impact which they make upon human capacity to respond to divine leading. The broad message of Scripture does not support the idea of Christianity as a mere spiritual Cape Canaveral, concerned solely to be a launching pad for heaven. God, to whom time and eternity are indivisible, affirms not "I did make" nor "I will make," but "I *make* all things new." And we are called to be co-laborers with God in a continuing divine metamorphosis as he brings forth the new.

An expectant father and I, sitting in a hospital room, heard the chilling call on the public-address system, "Calling all doctors to Maternity." While we sat in nervous uncertainty, his wife's delivery of a son and her survival were made possible by the assembling of the greatest possible concentration of obstetrical skills. When God brought forth something new in the long odyssey of human development in the eighteenth-century birth of this nation, he had assembled a team unmatched in human history.

They, in turn, had a sense of "God at work" in what they were doing. Humanists though some of them were, they spoke of that birth as taking place "under the laws of nature's God" and they performed the delivery of the infant nation "with a firm reliance on Divine Providence." We get a glimpse of men rooted in faith, leaning forward on tiptoe with expectancy as something new was born—under God. Through these twenty decades we have lived in the faith that in this nation God had, out of the old, made something new. We have believed that God presided over an event that might be described in the words of the astronaut stepping from the space vehicle to the surface of the moon: "One small step for a man, one giant leap for mankind."

With such an illustrious team having, under God, ushered into existence such an exciting "something new," why do we, two centuries later, talk about a "new birth of freedom?" Is a new birth of freedom possible? Is it necessary? The simple answer is that when we assume that we have exhausted God's dream we are guilty of blasphemy—a blasphemy that is challenged by God's ringing affirmation, "I make all things new!" A new birth is possible—yes!

More than that, a new birth is imperative. It is imperative because that all-star team made mistakes. It is imperative because each successive generation has done damage to God's eighteenth-century creation. It is imperative because an undreamed-of future comes crashing in upon us as God moves relentlessly in his world, creating new conditions without regard to man's readiness or willingness to meet them.

A new birth is imperative because the ability of that all-star team to perform a perfect delivery was hindered by their corporate nearsightedness. They had a vision of all men created equal, endowed by their Creator with inalienable rights. But their myopia blurred the image of the slave as a human being. Men who had the highest composite ideals then known to man, men who had suffered and were willing to suffer more for that bright new liberty, men who claimed inalienable rights from their Creator—were unable to rise above the politics of human greed and extend those God-given rights to all humanity. Thus they consigned generations to a living death. Thus they injected a deadly virus into the bloodstream of the infant nation that continued far past the proverbial third and fourth generation and that throws its foreboding shadow over this two hundredth birthday party and far down the future.

A new birth is imperative because of the cumulative effects of the failure of successive generations to approximate in reality the high ideals which were set forth by the Founding Fathers and to which they themselves gave lip service. Consistently through the generations property and profits—not people—were paramount. Let a series of flashbacks remind us of those betrayals. Our hands were bloodied with the major genocide of modern history as in clearing the land we cut down trees and Indians with equal carelessness . . . Many immigrants were welcomed by the Statue of Liberty only to be ruthlessly exploited as soon as they were behind the Fair Lady's back . . . Exploitation of children contributed to the fortunes of Christian "philanthropists" . . . Laboring people, wading in their own blood trying to organize, were castigated as subversives for insisting that the "sixth commandment of the Constitution"—to promote the general welfare—should have some substance. Some of these, having later secured their status, became a new generation of oppressors . . . Religious freedom, the avowed goal of many colonialists, was parodied in signs that read, "No dogs or Catholics allowed" . . . "All men are created equal" meant just what it said and equality for women is still an issue . . . Slavery, the deadly legacy of the Founding Fathers, died in a bloody birth of freedom, only for that freedom to exist to the present as a stunted, crippled thing . . . The Spanish-speaking people of the Southwest were brought into the nation at gunpoint and kept out of it the same way . . . Americans of Japanese ancestry were robbed of their freedom and property as late as 1942 and have not been requited for either . . . America sang of "the land of the free," while in its communities and clubs, its churches and its Congress, it guaranteed to millions of Americans of every color, including many whites, neither life, liberty, nor the pursuit of anything! These massive and persistent failures, extending to this day and occasionally breaking out in new and virulent forms, make a new birth of freedom imperative.

A new birth is imperative in order to open the nation up to the future that comes crashing in upon us. The Fathers severed the political umbilical cord with Europe. Fleeing from the centuries-old encrustations of Europe and fearing that they, too, should leap the seas and strangle that new freedom in its infancy, they rejected entangling alliances, withdrawing into their insular castle, with the sea as their protective moat. But step by step, shiploads of human or freight cargo one after another, war by war, a web has been woven, tying this nation not only with Europe but with all mankind. This planet-wide knitting process has culminated technologically in a weaver's shuttle of airborne traffic, politically in the fetal stage of world government in the United Nations, economically in the transnational corporation that can help to bring world freedom or to destroy it, and ecclesiastically in the World Council of Churches with the potential to supply the spiritual guidance and power without which the other world-unifying forces may well become demonic. The first birth was for living in near-isolation; the new birth must be for global living.

The catalog of failings listed here might seem to suggest that the earlier birth was a failure. That is not true. Although much of its rich potential has been tragically squandered, when the epic of these two centuries is set in the context of the sweep of history and even in the context of the totality of life on this planet today, its errors, however tragic in cause or consequence, can be seen as stumblings along the way toward the distant goal of freedom and justice.

The apostle John writes, "I am writing you no new commandment, but an old commandment which you had from the beginning" (I John 2:7). The nation heard a commandment two centuries ago and obeyed it in many ways that made this nation the example and champion of freedom. People swarmed from all over the world, escaping various restrictions on freedom, looking for the freedom written into America's birth certificate. When I inquired of African friends why they were so much more openly critical of the United States for its failings than they were of the Russians, they replied that they expected more of the United States, and so our moral lapses were more painful to them. There was an "old commandment" in that birth, and to a large extent, America "got the message."

That old commandment for freedom under God was obeyed as citizens struggled against the denials of freedom that were poisoning the body. They ranged from unknown and unsung people who pressed for changes, to a few giants who in literal or figurative martyrdom gave the body a transfusion by injecting the blood of their own sacrifices into purifying the bloodstream of the nation.

The old commandment was obeyed as, with faltering steps and often unworthy motives, the nation moved from its self-inflicted isolationism and began to "join the human race." An American president's dream of a League of Nations died in infancy but led the way for the birth of the United Nations. The Marshall Plan was the most massive Good Samaritan Act in history. The Foreign Aid program, although a mixture of goodwill and self-serving conniving, has held out a helping hand to developing nations in a way not seen before in history. We have occasionally sent military armies to various places around the world, but for more than a century we have maintained a consistent force abroad, armed with the gospel of Jesus Christ, carrying in his name literacy, health, development. That army has opened the doors to fuller life for millions and, although inadvertently, sowed the seed for the birth of new nations. There has truly been some obedience of the old commandment.

John continues, however, to say that he is, after all, writing a new commandment, because the movement from darkness toward the light creates new conditions (I John 2:8). In this nation the old commandment takes on a new meaning in the light of the new conditions God has created. The explosion of knowledge in the personal, social, natural, and medical sciences opens up to mankind new vistas for the individual and the society. The explosion of communication, travel, and economics creates new conditions that create a new commandment that calls for a new birth. Our capabilities of implementing President Franklin D. Roosevelt's Four Freedoms and still other freedoms are a new thing in the history of mankind.

The new commandment calls for a birth for global living. Freedom anywhere is tied to freedom everywhere. The Marshall Plan, Foreign Aid, the Missionary Movement, have been good starting points in obedience to the old commandment. But the old commandment could countenance war as a tool of civilized nations. The new commandment and the new conditions call for a birth free from war. Hunger has been the accepted lot of masses by themselves as well as by the well-fed. The new conditions and the new commandment demand a world without hunger. "No man is an island" has moved from poetry to stark reality, and the truth is pressing in upon us that freedom is indivisible.

What can the old birth of freedom teach us about the requisites for the new birth?

The eighteenth-century birth of freedom could occur because people opened themselves up to newness. They cut their ties with the old, the familiar, the comfortable, things, places, and even people whom they loved. A new birth under God cannot come to pass in the lives of people who cling tenaciously to yesterday, who can never reevaluate the old and the familiar. It cannot happen to those who are unwilling to sacrifice some status or privilege. It cannot happen to those who are unwilling to be uprooted. Christians often find themselves in an ambivalent position relative to change. We become so committed to our role as conservators of values that we resist our role in stimulating and guiding change. We fall into that blasphemous idea that we have exhausted God's dream for his world. Thus we are absent when new things are born rather than guiding the birth. God calls us to be a pioneer people always symbolically dwelling in tents.

The new nation could be born in a glorious new burst of freedom because people had a vision of something new, greater, finer. Shiploads of people moved to these shores because their occupants visualized some better world than they had known. True, many were seeking only quick wealth, but there were enough people of vision among them to spawn the dream of the new birth of freedom. The new birth of freedom to which God calls us today can come only to a people whose youth have visions and whose elderly dream dreams. It cannot come to those who are captives of their affluence, so drunk with their power and absorbed in their superficial enjoyments of life that their souls cannot be excited by God's distant possibilities. God calls his church to catch the reflection of the heavenly vision and lead in transforming the old into a continuously renewing "something new."

That earlier birth of freedom could happen because people were willing to risk the unknown for their dreams. There is no way for this generation to imagine the wrenching of spirit that it took for them to leave the known for the unknown. With our global knowledge we cannot conceive of the state of mind of those who sailed out into seas that many still thought ended in nothingness. Even the assurance of arrival, something that none of them had, could only guarantee their landing on some strange shore.

The new birth of freedom under God summons us toward strange shores and unfamiliar territories. We are called to reorganize our national life to cope with conditions that were beyond the wildest imaginings of the Founding Fathers. We are called to reshape economic practices and personal levels of consumption in order to share the earth's resources with our distant contemporaries and our distant offspring. We are called to carry the gospel into a world that changes with baffling rapidity. These and other imperatives for us are strange, frightening territory.

In short, that eighteenth-century birth of freedom took place because people were willing to live and die for it. God's commanded new birth of freedom can take place only when another generation is willing to pay the price God requires. Those for whom God is peripheral can never be the instruments of the new birth. Those who see God as a tool to be used by themselves cannot effectively be used by God. Those who are fenced in by the encrustations of race, class, or nation cannot catch the vision out of which the birth must come. New birth calls for people whose fervent prayer is, "Thy will be done . . . in me."

The Christian's involvement in the new birth in the nation is founded upon faith. The Fathers predicated their theories and actions upon the God of history. But the new birth must grow out of an expanded concept of God and of his will. Israel spoke of a God of heaven and earth, but in reality saw Jehovah as its tribal God, a concept that the nation had to outgrow. We have all the language of a God of the universe and of history, but that concept must become so vitally new that it eventuates in a new commandment for a new birth of freedom. God becomes the real basis for "One World" as our understanding of the fatherhood of God breaks down the man-made barriers that separate us and that permit a few of us to live in profligate splendor while those who are equally his children are enslaved by privations beyond our understanding. He is the God of all nations and does not function under the Stars and Stripes. He is the God who gave his Son in a shocking act of redemption, but gave him for all his creation. He is the God who will, if we are obedient and faithful, open up new worlds in human relations as he opens up new worlds in space. Truly, the eye has not seen nor the ear heard, nor has the mind of man conceived of the things that God has prepared for those who love him (I Cor. 2:9).

God calls us to be his co-workers in making all things new. God calls us to a veritable new birth of freedom . . . but under him!

15
When You Think You Have Had Enough

WILLIAM G. GILLESPIE
Cote Brilliante Presbyterian Church
St. Louis, Missouri

William Gillespie's ministry in St. Louis spans a period of twenty years. He went to his present parish as a fledgling minister after a one-year pastorate in the Davie Street Presbyterian Church in Raleigh, North Carolina.

Gillespie has held various offices in the judicatories of the region in which he lives. He was elected moderator of the Synod of Missouri in 1968, and moderator of the Presbytery of St. Louis in 1969. He has also served as a member of various committees.

His community involvement is extensive. It ranges from the presidency of the Board of Harris Teachers College to membership in OIC. This minister's community has shown its appreciation of his impact on both church and community by awarding him the Citizen of the Year Citation and the Distinguished Citizen Award.

William Gillespie was born in Knoxville, Tennessee. He is a graduate of Knoxville College and Johnson C. Smith Seminary.

The sermon "When You Think You Have Had Enough" was preached in the Cote Brilliante Church. It reveals the sermonic fare this preacher has been serving to his parishioners for a generation.

SERMON 15

It is enough.

I KINGS 19:4

When I was a boy, poverty for black people was real. Those were the days when there was no television and only a few persons owned radios. Many homes were without the bare necessities such as electricity and running water. Many families in our neighborhood would gather at the home of one of the few neighbors who owned a radio to listen to the broadcast of Joe Louis boxing. I remember listening to the fight in which Max Schmeling defeated Joe Louis. The reaction of all those gathered was one I shall never forget. It was as if their world had come to an end. Joe represented someone to be admired. He was a black man, and the best heavyweight boxer in the world. He epitomized the longing of black people in America to be the best. Each victory for Joe Louis was a victory for black America. Joe Louis gave hope to blacks in despair. If he could be the best in boxing and make people proud of him, then others could be the best in science, medicine, art, and a thousand other fields of endeavor. But that night Joe Louis was defeated.

Little did I know that one day I would experience this feeling of despair among black people again. It came upon the news of the assassination of Dr. Martin Luther King, Jr. Dr. King represented a man of whom all America could be proud. He refused to sacrifice principle for the sake of expediency. He would not close his eyes to the evils of racism and live as though they did not exist. No, he exposed racism, condemned segregation and discrimination of all forms, practiced love for all people—even his enemies. He would not declare that peace and harmony prevailed while he knew that the cancer of racial discrimination was gnawing away at the vitals of the nation. He attacked racism in an effort to destroy it. Dr. King exposed segregation in an effort to remove it from the scene. He opposed violence as a method of solving any problems. Some called him Black Moses. Others looked upon him as a messiah. Still others saw him as the only one with an answer to the American dilemma. But in April, 1968, the news came—"Dr. King is dead!" This shattered the hopes and dreams of us all. Like Elijah, we were ready to cry, "It is enough!"

Life is like that. The very moment your goal is in sight it turns you around and places your goal farther away. Or you become planted in some congenial soil, and along comes a rude gardener who uproots you and moves you on. We have often felt like that writer who declared: "Life is too great a journey; I cannot travel it trustingly. Life is too great a mission; I cannot live it helpfully. Life is too great a contest; I cannot live it victoriously. Life is too great a struggle; I cannot live it successfully. I have had enough."

Life is a journey in which too many of us give up. We begin with great enthusiasm. We trust that we will reach our goal. We have a heart and mind for a successful journey, but soon we are confronted by roadblocks which seem to make that journey impossible. Elijah knew what it meant to be confronted by a roadblock. His was in the form of a woman named Jezebel. This man, tired and spent, had passed through exacting circumstances. Many were his worries prior to his test on Mt. Carmel. Would God vindicate his faith? Would God cause his adversaries to really know that he was His true servant? In other words, would God be on time with His help when it would be needed? Elijah discovered that God was on time. Look at the picture. Ahab has assembled four hundred and fifty prophets of Baal on Mt. Carmel. This was done at the request of Elijah, who wanted the people to make a choice between God and Baal. Almost every student of the Bible can recall his challenge to the people: "How long halt ye between two opinions? if the Lord be God, follow him: but if Baal, then follow him." This was a great moment for both Israel and Elijah. There was silence, no answer when Elijah made his challenge. If silence means consent, then it would appear that the people were pledging their allegiance to the Lord God of Israel. This is not sufficient for Elijah. He wants to hear from their mouths, "The Lord, he is God."

Elijah explains the rules of the contest that is to take place between Baal and God. Following these rules, the prophets of Baal built an altar, killed a bullock, cut it up and laid it on the wood of the altar. They were instructed to put no fire under the altar. The priests of Baal would call upon their god to supply fire, and then Elijah would call upon the God of Israel to do the same. The god who answered by fire would be God. One can almost see the priests of Baal circling the altar, dancing around the sacrifice from morning to noon. They entreat Baal: "Hear us! Hear us!" But Baal is just as silent as the people were to Elijah's challenge. Elijah makes sport of them. He seems to get a thrill from it all, seeing them cut themselves with knives, inflicting physical wounds that would take a long time to heal, trying their best to convince everyone they were doing all they could to make their god hear and answer. But their god remained silent.

Now it is Elijah's turn. He calls the people to come near. Then the prophet with twelve stones repaired a broken-down altar. He dug a trench about the altar and placed the sacrifice, a slain bullock, upon the wood. Four jars of water were poured over the sacrifice upon the wood three times. The water ran around the altar and filled the trench.

It is time for Elijah to call upon God to consume the sacrifice with fire. Listen to his prayer: "O Lord, God of Abraham, Isaac, and Israel, let it be known this day that thou art God in Israel, and that I am thy servant, and that I have done all these things at thy word. Answer me, O Lord, answer me, that this

people may know that thou, O Lord, art God, and that thou
hast turned their hearts back." Then the fire of the Lord fell,
and consumed the burnt offering and the wood, and the stones,
and the dust, and licked up the water that was in the trench.
When the people saw what had happened, they fell on their
faces and said, "The Lord, he is God." After his victory, Elijah
had the prophets of Baal seized and killed.

Ahab saw Elijah's prayers for both fire and rain answered.
On their return to Jezreel, Elijah was so happy over his victories
that he ran before Ahab. When Ahab came into the presence
of Jezebel, he told her all that Elijah had done, and how he had
slain all the prophets with the sword. Then Jezebel sent a
messenger to Elijah saying, "So may the gods do to me, and
more also, if I do not make your life as the life of one of them
by this time tomorrow."

This threat was something Elijah could not cope with. It
took away the sweetness of his victory and filled him with
anxiety. He became so fearful of Jezebel that it drove him to
madness. He eventually ended up in the wilderness. So frustrat-
ing was his experience that it took much of his physical
strength away. The Book of First Kings records it this way: "He
. . . went a day's journey into the wilderness, and came and sat
down under a broom tree; and he asked that he might die,
saying, 'It is enough; now, O Lord, take away my life; for I am
no better than my fathers.' "

There are times when many of us become weary. We represent causes that are good, but no good comes from our work.
We support people who give themselves relentlessly to a good
cause and they are killed, imprisoned, or silenced by the forces
of evil. We knock on doors that are closed to black people until
our knuckles are raw, but the doors remain closed. We prepare
ourselves for jobs we never get, for housing we cannot buy, for
clubs we cannot enter, for churches where we are unwanted,
for dreams that never come true. There are times when we all
feel like crying, "I've had enough; I can't take any more." But
when you think you have had enough, remember that the race

isn't given to the swift, but to him who endures to the end. Remember the words of James, "Happy is the man who remains faithful under trials."

Many of you will recall the movie that was quite popular in the '40s. It was entitled *Stormy Weather*. One of the stars was Lena Horne, and she sang the title song. In her song she described her discouragement as a result of being separated from the man she loved. Poignant are the words—"keeps on raining all the time. I can't go on; everything I had is gone!" That's the way many felt when Dr. King was assassinated, and when Joe Louis was defeated. Surely this was the feeling of Elijah when he declared, "It is enough."

Elijah felt discouraged because he did not believe that he was a match for Jezebel. This led him to believe that he was inferior in other things. He looked about and lost faith in his fellowman. Elijah did not feel that he could recruit forces strong enough to overcome Jezebel, and he felt that no one else could either.

So many black Americans had this feeling upon King's death. Yet, thank God, it was not King's feeling while he was alive. He said, "I may not get to the promised land with you, but one day we as a people will get there!" He lived with a buoyant optimism. He would not let disappointment, fear, or frustration turn him around. He knew that challenges must be met with our best effort and God's help. He knew that throwing up our hands, walking out on our dreams, screaming, "I've had enough!" would never help one reach his goal. Men must be willing to risk danger, suffer, if it is needful, and even die to achieve some goals. Have we forgotten those blacks faced with discouragement in slavery? They sang such songs of encouragement as "I'll Never Turn Back No More," "Children, Don't You Get Weary," and that comforting spiritual from which these words come:

There is a balm in Gilead
  To make the wounded whole,
There is a balm in Gilead

> To heal the sin-sick soul.
> Sometimes I feel discouraged,
>   And think my work's in vain,
> But then the Holy Spirit
> Revives my soul again.

When you think you have had enough, just tell yourself that you can take a little bit more. Tell yourself that you are the equal to your discouragement. The words of an old adage declare, "We can't prevent birds from flying over our heads, but we can prevent them from making nests in our hair." Discouragements are sure to come our way, but we need not let them defeat us. Who among us hasn't been discouraged? Our Lord knew discouragement. Surely in the Garden of Gethsemane he was discouraged by his disciples as they slept while he prayed. He expressed it in his words: "Are you still sleeping and taking your rest? Behold, the hour is at hand, and the Son of man is betrayed into the hands of sinners." And yet, how swiftly he challenges even those who had discouraged him. "Rise, let us be going."

Recall again Elijah and his discouragement. Was he defeated by it? What did he do to overcome it? Was he so mesmerized by things that he continued to sit weeping under the broom tree? The words of the writer of the Book of First Kings are these: "And he lay down and he slept under a broom tree; and behold, an angel touched him." I like these words. They show us the importance of rest if one is to perform at his best. One who receives adequate rest is better equipped to deal with his problems than those who do not. Elijah was awakened by the touch of an angel. This was indicative of the fact that God was present with him. Elijah now had no need to think himself helpless in the face of his circumstances. He set out on a journey of forty days and nights into a wilderness. Coming to a cave, he heard the voice of God: "What doest thou here, Elijah?" Without hesitation, Elijah makes his position known: "I have been very jealous for the Lord God of hosts: for the children of Israel have forsaken thy covenant, thrown down thine altars, and slain thy prophets with the sword; and I, even

I only, am left; and they seek my life, to take it away." Recall the Lord's response. It was a great and strong wind that rent the mountains, and broke in pieces the rocks. The Lord was not in the wind nor the earthquake which followed, nor the fire that came after that. God spoke to Elijah in a still, small voice.

The Lord gave him a new perspective on life and a new vision of God. God let Elijah know that all was well as far as Israel's religion was concerned. God put Elijah to work again. He had a great task which needed to be performed, and Elijah was God's man to do it. He spent the remainder of his life doing good—anointing kings, choosing a successor to himself, and, I am sure, praising God.

A number of years ago I came across the story of a young man who lost a leg while serving in the United States Armed Forces. He never lost his beautiful outlook on life. "This is a temporary setback," he wrote his mother. "But I will succeed in spite of it." Each of us is called to make the most of life in whatever circumstances we find ourselves. We must believe we can overcome. We must make all our defeats temporary.

In the beginning I told you of Joe Louis' defeat. He made it a temporary setback. There was a second fight between Louis and Schmeling. Joe won the second fight by a knockout in the first round. From that temporary setback he went on to become one of the greatest heavyweight champions of all time. So often after his victories his words would be similar to these: "I am glad I won. God was on my side." The hymn writer put it this way:

> Be still, my soul: the Lord is on thy side;
>   Bear patiently the cross of grief or pain;
> Leave to thy God to order and provide;
>   In every change he faithful will remain.
>
> Be still, my soul: thy God doth undertake
>   To guide the future as he has the past.
> Thy hope, thy confidence, let nothing shake;
>   All now mysterious shall be bright at last.

Hugh Walpole wrote: "It is not life that matters. It is the courage you bring to it." So, when we come to that point in life where we think we've had enough, we need to reflect on the lines of those who have refused to be defeated by discouragement. Bring a positive attitude into this situation. Don't give way to self-pity. This ultimately leads to failure and defeat. We must not become bitter or resentful for the circumstances in which we find ourselves. Refuse to accept the situation as final and turn your disadvantages into advantages. In other words, make the most of your situation.

Dr. Clarence Macartney told the story of an old man with a bundle of sticks on his back. He sank down by the roadside, and with a groan said he wished he were dead. To his surprise and terror, Death at once made his appearance and asked him what he would have. The old man said quickly, "My bundle on my back, and my feet once more on the road." In his discouragement, what he asked for was not really what he desired. This is true of many of our wishes in the hour of discouragement.

Some will say this all seems too naive. For people who have been waiting so long for a better day, this is understandable. We must live with a long-term faith. Of course, we would like to see things happen now. We must work to make things happen now. All of us want to achieve our goals, realize our dreams while we are here on earth. We must not let a temporary setback stop us. We must keep on keeping on! We must undertake great adventures and challenge others to do the same. Our dreams for justice, equality, and true freedom must remain alive! Jesus lived in this spirit. He spoke of the coming of the kingdom of God. He did not see it. He believed that it would come, and because he believed so strongly that it would become a reality, he suffered and died on the cross.

Each of us can learn from Jesus' experience. What are your personal discouragements? What makes you want to give up? For each the discouragements are similar—unemployment, soaring death rate from strokes and heart attacks among blacks, repeated failures with our children and sometimes our marriages. But we must continue on. We must continue to work in whatever capacity we find ourselves. Your work is needed. You may not be a senator, representative, state legislator, or mayor. You may not hold any public office—but your work is needed. Your work in your home church and community may be the humblest of all tasks—but it is needed! Put your heart and mind in it. Let nothing stop you or turn you around. This is no time for throwing in the towel. You cannot afford to say, "I've had enough; I can't take any more."

In this sermon I have sought to describe to you how different individuals have handled discouragements, some much greater than any of us would ever encounter. Joe Louis, Dr. Martin Luther King, Jr., Elijah, and even Jesus Christ—all faced discouragement, but each felt his work or cause was so important that he refused to be defeated. With the faith and knowledge that God the Father would see them through, they accomplished what they had to do. With this same faith, we can do it too.

16
What a Way to Live

ELIAS S. HARDGE, JR.
West End Presbyterian Church
Atlanta, Georgia

Elias Hardge's conviction is that the black preacher's experience enables him to bring "a quality of soul that lifts the declaration of the gospel to a new dimension" in the Presbyterian Church. This conviction motivates Elias to engage regularly in complete and careful sermon preparation.

"What a Way to Live" reflects the results of this discipline. It was delivered at Emory University in Atlanta, Georgia, shortly after the assassination of Dr. Martin Luther King, Jr.

Hardge was born in Indianapolis, Indiana, and studied at New York University, the University of Connecticut, North Carolina Central University, and Candler School of Theology. He was ordained in the Freemont Methodist Episcopal Zion Church and served congregations in New York, Connecticut, and North Carolina. His record of service includes adjunct faculty membership at McCormick Theological Seminary and Columbia Theological Seminary.

In 1971 Elias Hardge was called to the West End Presbyterian Church. Atlanta has felt the impact of his preaching. That city is also profiting from his leadership in a variety of community endeavors.

For whoever would save his life will lose it; and whoever loses his life for my sake, he will save it.

LUKE 9:24

He leaned over the balcony of the second floor of the Lorraine Hotel, just outside his room, to be able to hear words being spoken from below by the Rev. Jesse Jackson. Jesse said, "Doc, this is Ben Branch, the musician who is going to play for our rally tonight." "Yes," King answered, "Branch is my man." "Be sure to play 'Precious Lord,' Brother Branch. Be sure to play it pretty."

It was as he straightened up that it happened. The shot, soon to be echoed around the world, was fired. Martin Luther King, Jr., fell, never to rise again in this world, at least, under his own power. He lay there, with his legs draped over the railing, eyes in a death stare, spinal cord severed, as life oozed out of him in a pool of blood.

Someone said, during those early hours of agony, "My God, what a way to die." Given time for reflection, someone else said, "What a way to live!"

All of us have developed or are in the process of developing a life-style. In the final analysis the life-style we adopt will have something to do with that which is ultimate for each of us. We will die or we will live.

How does a man choose his *modus operandi?* Where does a man look to find a pattern for his life-style? This question has important implications for those of us who are concerned about the conclusion of the whole matter of life.

Our text provides us with a means of choosing our style of living. The text says, "For whoever would save his life will lose it; and whoever loses his life for my sake, he will save it." It is quite possible that in these words there is something of value for those of us, in the community of faith, who are struggling to find meaning in our existence in this twentieth-century jungle in which we live. Perhaps there is a saving word from the Lord in the text as we consider the *life-style we choose.*

Life-styles are developed primarily around the acquiring and preserving of things that have meaning for us. It is possible that we can become so obsessed with holding on to that which is precious to us that we lose it. Our text puts it this way, "For whoever would save his life will lose it." In other words, the life-style we choose can lead to the loss of life. Our preoccupation with saving life could lead to the loss of it.

Recently, three men traveled to the moon and back. Their safe return depended upon their giving strict attention to plans and procedures that had been worked out far in advance of the trip. If at any given point, these men had become obsessed with their own safety, the chances are they would not have been able to fly to the moon, gather up moon samples, and return safely to earth. Their safe return depended upon their concentration upon the moon mission objective.

Life-styles are not peculiar to individuals. Nations develop life-styles which tend to preserve them or destroy them. As we look at this nation of ours today, one cannot help wondering if perhaps we have chosen not to live.

Life depends on wholeness and unity. This nation is afflicted with several illnesses which undermine its general health.

There are institutions and people in our midst who are afflicted with neolotry (worship of the new), as Ernest Campbell puts it. They respond to contemporary pressures by absolutizing change. They operate on the philosophy that anything new is better than anything old.

There are others of us who are afflicted with bigness worship. They/we have fallen prey to the mistaken notion that if you've got the biggest, you've got the best. If our bomb has more megatons than Russia's bombs, we are superior. Oh, how we need to realize that

> Bigger is not better;
> Slower may be faster;
> Less may well mean more.

There are others of us who are afflicted with an illness that makes a god out of technology. They/we are laboring under the false illusion that science is on the way to being able to answer all our questions, solve all our problems.

There is another illness that pervades this nation. It is an illness that is more encompassing and life threatening than all the others. It is an illness that has reached epidemic proportions. For a long time its proper diagnosis eluded us. Because of incorrect diagnosis, wrong medications were prescribed; therefore, no cure was affected. Minority people and the ghetto were the problem, it was said. But finally, at long last, a correct diagnosis has been made. The illness was found to be white racism, and it is everywhere. It has our nation divided and if a house be divided, it cannot stand; it cannot live; it will die. White racism, that combination of attitudes, structure, and behavior patterns which has systematically subordinated dark-skinned minorities in both church and society; white racism, identified by the Kerner Commission report and largely ignored, for the most part, by the governing powers of this nation.

Blacks and other nonwhites are alienated by white racism because every institution, every assumption in American life, including the Christian church, supports and keeps white racism alive and well. Even at this late hour of history, the white church is reluctant to grant blacks full status, is unwilling to use its rich material resources to empower black people, and spends most of its energies defending its privileged position in society. While the white church has been involved in the contemporary civil rights struggle, it still remains a racist institution, even where it has black leadership. It has been reluctant to trust black leadership, clergy and lay. There are congregations all over this nation that have signed their death warrant by their refusal to minister to a part of their community that happens to be black. I'm talking about choosing a style of life that leads to death.

The man whose memory we honor here today looked at his country and looked at the body of Christ, of which he was a part, and saw that the life-style chosen by them had them headed on a road leading to death. Martin Luther King, Jr., took seriously the mission of Jesus in the world. Apparently, he had been exposed to the mandate of Jesus as recorded in Luke 4:18: "The Spirit of the Lord is upon me, because he has anointed me to preach good news to the poor. He has sent me to proclaim release to the captives and recovering of sight to the blind, to set at liberty those who are oppressed, to proclaim the acceptable year of the Lord." Under that mandate Martin Luther King, Jr., set out, a voice crying in this twentieth-century wilderness.

Yes, the life-style we choose may lead to a loss of life—Jesus attacked the evils of his day and wound up on a cross on top of a garbage heap in Jerusalem. He had hoped the coming of the kingdom would be accomplished by a bloodless revolution, but a crown of thorns caused blood to run down the cross, a spear in his side caused blood to saturate the earth. Martin Luther King had hoped that the coming of the kingdom could or would be accomplished by a bloodless revolution and he wound up in a pool of his own blood on top of a garbage heap in Memphis.

The life-style we choose can lead to death. What a dismal, gloomy, bloody, depressing picture of human hopelessness. If it ended here, what a waste; Jesus the savior of the world, hanging lifeless on a cross. Martin Luther King, Jr., his disciple, lying lifeless on a balcony. Thank God this morning, their stories don't end there.

Our text tells us that we have another option. There is another style of living that will result in the saving of life. The

text says, "Whoever loses his life for my sake, he will save it."
There is, then, the possibility that the *life-style we choose can
lead to life*.

Any institution that expects to live and that is truly concerned about living does something about insuring life. There
is a periodic reevaluation of procedures and policies and practices to see whether or not it is continuing to move in the
direction of its goals and objectives.

What is it we're striving for? The concern of our text is life.
It seems paradoxical that this particular part of the text seems
to say if you really want to save your life, give it away, yet this
is precisely what it is saying. There is an unexplainable mysteri-
ousness that makes possible the keeping of that which one gives
away.

It is important here, in considering this other option, that
we consider it completely. The text does not say simply, Whoever loses his life will save it. It says, Whoever loses his life
for my sake will save it. This is the Lord of all life speaking.
A wanton disregard for life, a senseless disregard for life, will
not result in saving life. But when given for Him, the picture
is different. It is this putting of our text in proper perspective
that concerns us now.

It is high time for our nation to reevaluate itself, if it is to
live. There are a couple of lies that have been circulating in our
midst for years and years. If you're fortunate enough to have
a piece of money in your pocket, take a look at it—the words
"In God We Trust" and "E Pluribus Unum" ("one from
many"). We have made such a mockery of things that should
be surrounded with sacredness.

I wonder what would happen if we took seriously the Christian principles upon which this nation was founded? What
would happen if we really trusted in God, instead of stockpiles
of nuclear weapons, guided missiles, and white superiority?
What would happen if we took seriously the admonition of
Jesus about losing our lives for his sake? Jesus said, "Whoever
loses his life for my sake, he will save it." But will he?

Martin Luther King, Jr., believed that Jesus meant what he

said. Being convinced of that, as he looked at the human situation in the light of the message of Jesus, he started to challenge his nation to live up to its Christian commitment. There was something about the manner of this twentieth-century prophet that was disturbing to those who resisted the mandate of the gospel. As Jesus set his face steadfastly toward Jerusalem, so King set his face steadfastly toward oppression. He believed that there was a style of life that led to life, even though it appeared to lead to death.

The night before he was killed, apparently an angel of the Lord strengthened him, in the same way our Lord had been strengthened in Gethsemane. Listen to the words of Martin after his Gethsemane:

> We've got some difficult days ahead—but it really doesn't matter with me now—I've been to the mountaintop. I won't mind. Like anybody I'd like to live a long life. Longevity has its place—but I'm not concerned about that now—I just want to do God's will—And He's allowed me to go to the mountain—I've looked over—I've seen the promised land. . . . I'm happy tonight, mine eyes have seen the glory of the coming of the Lord.

It seems, many times, that tragedy follows on the heels of triumphs. Today the roaring crowds—tomorrow a bullet on a balcony in the middle of a garbage strike. Today the roaring crowds—tomorrow a cross on top of a garbage heap.

Martin got a bullet in the head because he was crazy enough to believe that a man who loses his life for Jesus will save it. Did it end on a balcony in Memphis? I think not. Let's examine the Gospel. Jesus bucked the establishment. When things got too hot for them they decided to kill him. They gave him a trial that was a joke. Pilate manuevered things so he wouldn't have blood on his hands. They marched Jesus up a hill called Calvary. They nailed him to a cross. They laid him in a tomb. They placed a stone in front of the tomb to make sure Jesus was permanently entombed. But they tell me early on Easter morning; early, while the dew was still on the roses; early, before the birds had started their singing; early, before God reached up with his ethereal hand and lifted the curtain of night, God sent an angel to roll the stone away and Jesus emerged conqueror over death, hell, and the grave.

Jesus said, "I am the resurrection, and the life: he that believeth in me, though he were dead, yet shall he live." Jesus also said, "Be thou faithful unto death, and I will give thee a crown of life." Martin was faithful unto death. He adopted a life-style of Jesus' that led to life through death.

Yes, there is a life-style which on the surface does not appear to lead to life at all.

The hours are long—The pay, by worldly standards, is totally inadequate—There will be many sleepless nights—What a way to live.

The road is lonely—The problems are overwhelming—The perplexities are many, the frustrations endless—What a way to live.

There may be a Gethsemane—There may be a Calvary—There will be a cross—There will be a grave—What a way to live.

No madman's bullet can stop the march for human rights; no murder, however tragic, can make it falter. In death, as in life, the words and spirit of this fallen leader will continue to inspire and lead us ever closer toward fulfillment of the ideals of domestic brotherhood and international peace. There is a life-style that leads from life to life. The question we leave you with today is: Can you commit yourself to this lifesaving life-style? What a way to live!

17
Golgotha 1964

FRANK T. WILSON
Oxford, Pennsylvania

Frank Wilson was born in Maxton, North Carolina. He grew up in Greensboro and Wadesboro, North Carolina. He is a graduate of Lincoln University, Pennsylvania, and Columbia University.

He began his professional career as National Student Secretary of the YMCA. This was followed by a thirteen-year period of service as dean of men and professor of education and psychology, Lincoln University, Pennsylvania.

From Lincoln University, Frank Wilson went to Howard University as dean of the School of Religion. After this he worked on the staff of the Commission on Ecumenical Mission and Relations of The United Presbyterian Church in the United States of America and the Commission on Theological Education in the Southeast.

Wilson's training and experiences eminently qualified him to serve as a consultant in education in this country and in Asia. He has also worked with secondary schools, colleges, universities, and theological seminaries in Africa, Latin America, and the Middle East.

Frank Wilson is a noted lecturer, writer, and preacher. The sermon "Golgotha 1964" reflects the thoroughness of his preparation, the skillful way he brings fresh insights to current events and applies the great themes of the Bible to them.

"Golgotha 1964" was written in Djakarta, Indonesia, November 7, 1963. It was and is Frank Wilson's message to the church in the United States of America.

SERMON 17

And when they were come to the place, which is called Calvary, there they crucified him, and the malefactors, one on the right hand, and the other on the left.

Luke 23:33

He was rejected, tormented, afflicted. In the moment of his deepest agony, he was ridiculed, reviled, forsaken. They nailed him to the cross. He died. Those who cared most ran away. Those who cared least have bequeathed a legacy of hostility to all for which he lived and to all for which he was willing to die —the incarnation of the love of God in the heart and life of humanity.

The most embarrassing chapter in the history of the church in the United States of America is the record of its behavior in the matter of racial discrimination and segregation. The more respectable the congregation, the more ingenious the devices of racial bigotry. The more affluent the pillars of the church, the more efficient the screening of "undesirables." In this process of preserving the purity of the faithful, race and color have been touchstones of acceptance or rejection.

Some voices are heard today, speaking in the name of religion, arguing that the easily distinguishable marks of race and color were established in creation and that these are badges of separation fully sanctioned in the design of the Creator. It is argued, furthermore, that anyone who attempts to alter the design tampers with the handiwork of God and is subject to his wrath. The absurdity of this contention is matched by the avidity with which it is absorbed by many who rummage through the Scriptures for Biblical justification of bigotry and racism.

Barely less pathetic are the more genteel and sophisticated rationalizations of the "churchly elite." This embraces the rank and file of American Protestantism who flee to the inverted ghetto of suburbia or extend a grudging crumb of tokenism within the stable, old-line urban churches. In either case the etiquette of human association is narrowly conditioned by restraints and taboos which magnify the formalities of membership without deepening and extending the experience of unqualified community within the fellowship of those who profess the Lordship of Christ over the totality of human life.

In many ways there is coldness and blindness and hardness within the church which exceeds the more crass and unpretentious rejections and humiliations of the secular world. This is felt more deeply because the idea of participation in the body of Christ has suggested a kind of relationship in which there is nothing which prevents the outgoing of the human spirit in a complete sharing of life at its most fundamentally significant levels. The witness to the world is validated by the living testimony before the world.

But the disastrous consequences of our faltering over the stumbling block of race is a sin so deeply engrained in the structures to which we pay allegiance and to which we make so many concessions that the way of deliverance appears to require more drastic measures than we can bear. Segregation and discrimination as manifestations of racism have so corroded the human spirit and so tarnished the soul that the acids of redemption threaten the very existence of the structures which they are designed to save.

The major tragedy of many Christian churches and individual Christians in America is not that they have denied membership to blacks and not welcomed them into their pews and pulpits and choirs and homes, but that these denials have issued from a basic *negation* of *life* and a willful *rejection of a portion of God's creation.* This negation has been so deep and so thoroughgoing that the church has been reluctant in seeking the way of repentance and in fulfilling the conditions of forgiveness and reconciliation.

The testimony of the church at one point on the globe conditions its capacity for revealing and mediating the love of God at any point on the globe. If fear, prejudice, and arrogance have rendered the church in America incapable of being the redeeming society in which black Americans share its full life in decency, quality, and full community, then it is unlikely that a spirit so distorted can bring health and healing to that which is deepest in the hearts of black, brown, red, yellow people in any part of the world. Charity, humanitarian services, and passionate evangelism may bring temporary relief and a measure of hope to persons in distress and physical anguish. But love that knows no bounds, that enriches our companionship with every child of God, is the only power that touches one's deepest yearning, the only force that reaches one's deepest need.

The church as a "community in mission" is composed of all those in every land who have professed allegiance to Jesus Christ as Lord and Savior and who have committed themselves to the fulfillment of the ethical and moral imperatives of the gospel. The church as an instrument of redemption in the world is confronted with the unavoidable demand to demonstrate in its own life that depth and breadth of fellowship and communion which destroys all walls of separation and which rejects all artificial and arbitrary barriers to human association.

In the mission of the church morality cannot be selective, ethical concern cannot be partial, zeal for freedom, equality, and justice cannot be conditioned by considerations of class or ethnic origins. Neither can Christians in America "play safe" or compromise on the issues of racial segregation and discrimination in this country, in our own communities and churches, without losing spiritual insight and moral courage so necessary for a sincere and genuine witness in the total world community.

There is a law of the spirit and a law of the mind which

makes it impossible for integrity to grow out of duplicity. I cannot at one and the same time be true to my neighbor in Asia and betray my neighbor in Africa. I cannot disrespect the dignity of my brothers and sisters in North America and honor the inherent worth of my brothers and sisters in Latin America.

There is no selective morality for the Christian which exempts one from recognizing the image of the Creator in every member of the human family, in all places of God's creation. It is a great illusion to suppose that the church or the individual Christian in the United States can live in convenient accommodation to the patterns of racial estrangement at home and then, or at the same time, participate with full conscience in building up the "beloved community" in Asia or Africa. There are evidences that evasiveness and cowardice in one situation undercut the capacity for resolute action in other situations containing similar factors. The obedience of the church as an instrument of reconciliation and unity in the world is dependent upon the preservation of its capacity for integrity in every local and national situation.

The mission of the church in America and in the world is indivisible. There is an underlying unity in life which is violated whenever offense is done to any segment of life. The yearning of the human spirit is not merely for houses and jobs and food and schools and votes, but basically for affirmation of worthfulness and identification with fellow human beings in all the high endeavors for fullness of life. The church is called to incarnate this ideal and to lead the way in America and to the end of the earth.

The madness of man is being tempered by the wisdom of God. The Holy Spirit is working in the affairs of this nation and in the life of the church as a mighty, moving wind and as a still, small voice. Men may hesitate, resist, and turn aside from the divine purpose, but what has been created in love and sustained by the indomitable will of the Maker of heaven and earth cannot be destroyed nor permanently defeated by the powers of evil at large in the world.

Where the church has conformed to the divisive forces in

society, where it has made cowardly concessions to pride or prejudice or bigotry, it stands under the judgment of Him who has made man in His own image and it betrays Him who looked upon the people of God with the agonizing prayer "that they all may be one." The possibility of the redemption of the church in its mission to the world becomes most apparent when all who profess faith in Jesus Christ as Lord recognize that we are no longer aliens or strangers, but fellow citizens with the saints and members of the household of God.

Every crucifixion is a universal event. Yet His love is boundless and His kingdom is an everlasting kingdom. The people of God *will enter their inalienable heritage.* Although the powers of hell may be arrayed against it.

18
You're O.K.—I'm O.K.

JAMES H. COSTEN
Johnson C. Smith Theological Seminary
Atlanta, Georgia

James Costen is recognized in Presbyterian circles as a successful recruiter of students for the professional ministry. To his students and colleagues at the Interdenominational Theological Center in Atlanta, Georgia, he is the beloved dean of Johnson C. Smith Theological Seminary.

What is not as widely known is the fact that Dean Costen is an effective preacher. He has the skill to tell the old story in new and fascinating ways. He knows how to apply eternal verities to current events. The sermon "You're O.K.—I'm O.K." demonstrates how he can apply homiletical skills to a current topic and theme. It was preached in the Mary Dod Brown Memorial Chapel, Lincoln University, Pennsylvania.

Costen's birthplace is Omaha, Nebraska. He is a graduate of Johnson C. Smith College and Seminary and Southeastern Theological Seminary.

He began his professional career as pastor of Mount Pisgah Presbyterian Church in Rocky Mount, North Carolina. Following this, he accepted a call to become organizing minister of the Church of the Master, Atlanta, Georgia.

Dean Costen has served on various presbytery, synod, and General Assembly councils and committees. He is chairperson of the Board of Harbison Development Corporation, Columbia, South Carolina, a new town development.

Costen has traveled in Germany, East Africa, West Africa, Egypt, France, England, and the Caribbean.

And Jesus said unto him, This day is salvation come to this house, forasmuch as he also is a son of Abraham.

LUKE 19:9

As Jesus passed through Jericho on his way to Jerusalem and his last appearance there, he came upon a large crowd that had heard of his works and wanted to see him. In that crowd was a man named Zacchaeus who was a rich tax collector. Tax collectors, then and now, are not particularly popular. Zacchaeus had gouged the people and had charged them unconscionably high taxes.

Zacchaeus was a man possessing many personal needs. He too wanted to see Jesus but did not feel wanted or appreciated by the crowd from whom he had previously collected taxes. Zacchaeus went ahead of the crowd, climbed into a tree, and found himself a vantage point on the limb of the tree. From his perch he could satisfy his intense desire to see Jesus and at the same time preserve his dignity and anonymity. From his tree limb Zacchaeus could avoid the barbs and the ostracism of the crowd. Here he could be safe.

Zacchaeus' actions are not unlike ours. We too, intentionally or unintentionally, climb our own trees and crawl out onto our tree limbs seeking safety from our feelings of real or imagined fears. Just as he did with Zacchaeus, Jesus invites us down from our hang-ups. Come down, he says, and let us, together, take a look at the problem. Together, let us seek the solution.

It was Jesus' perception that recognized Zacchaeus' predicament. Jesus knew that Zacchaeus desired to be with the crowd in authentic relationship. He knows also that we today want and need to be involved in authentic relationships but somehow cannot bring ourselves to do so because of our fears of being hurt. We want to protect ourselves from the pain of withdrawal. It appears easier to withdraw than to be hurt.

Many have problems with alcohol, with drugs, with sex, with socioeconomic exclusivism, and with religious status. Man is plagued by all kinds of hang-ups. It is fair to assume that, given an alternative, most people would prefer to rid themselves of their hang-ups, feelings of isolation, rejection, and fear.

Jesus knows our needs. He invites us to come down from whatever obstacles to which we are tenaciously clinging. To the boy or girl caught in the drug habit, Jesus says, Turn loose that limb and come down. To the man or woman seeking freedom from reality by drowning their sorrow in alcohol, Jesus says, Turn loose your crutch and find peace and fulfillment in him and other men.

To the person who feels that he is less important because of a lack of material possessions, Jesus says, Turn loose and climb down to the truth that it is not what a man has that makes him important but, rather, what a man is.

To those who are hung up thinking that they are better than others because of their educational or financial status, Jesus says, Not so. Seek your status in people, in causes, in religion. That which a man has can be here today and gone tomorrow. Relationships with Him and others are lasting.

Jesus is saying to all the Zacchaeuses of the world, Come down, turn loose your reliance on artificial security. Come on down and let us address the real issues.

When Jesus invites us down from our positions of insecurity, he offers us the possibility of addressing our needs at their very source—at home where we live. Jesus said to Zacchaeus, "Come down; for I must stay at your house today."

First of all, can't you imagine the exhilaration and throbbing of Zacchaeus' heart? A tax collector, hated by the crowds for his shady deals, having his name called by the object of his affection. Goose pimples must have welled up on his body. On many occasions we have not enjoyed the pleasure of having our names called. Black people have been called "boy," "nigger," "hey you," "uncle," "auntie," and many other names not appropriate for these pages. To be recognized, to have our names called, is important to all of us. Jesus not only calls us by name but invites himself into our "holy of holies," our most intimate dwelling, our walled and protected sanctuaries, into our very lives.

This is no idle gesture on his part. In a man's home, his castle, more than in any other place, all the masks of his being are stored, all the facade and pretensions tucked away. Where we live is our one bastion of security. Into such an intimate place Jesus invites himself.

The events in recent years attest to the fact that affluence and wasteful technology have not gone to the core of man's basic need. In fact, they have exacerbated his need. Sociology and psychiatry are increasingly coming to believe the basic and therapeutic value of Christianity. You see, Jesus allows us to be stripped to our inmost being without the disapproving glare of our own stares or those of others. He gives us the freedom and the courage to come to know the real person deep within. Most often we come to like that person when we get to know him better.

Jesus is desirous of going home with us today. Into the core of the city or into the most plush suburb, he is anxious to go there and to free us to truly be ourselves.

In spite of the fact that the invitation to be free is given to all, some will reject it and criticize you for accepting it. Some will criticize those who offer you freedom. There were those in the crowd who grumbled and were taken aback because Jesus offered to go home with Zacchaeus. "He has gone home to be the guest of a tax collector and sinner," they intoned.

We have but to see the attacks heaped upon Martin Luther King, Jr., for seeking to lead America and the world out of the darkness of personal and institutional racism into the light of a truly open society. His purpose was that America maximize the talents and contributions of all its people, north and south, rich and poor, nobly born or humbly born.

We have the example of many black people today who have been so victimized that they have become paranoid in their fear of all leadership, white or black. Many would rather "curse the darkness" than step into the light. Legitimate and sincere efforts at addressing certain problems are thwarted because of this lack of trust.

Let's not fool ourselves. To accept the freedom Jesus offers is demanding and threatening. It is demanding in that it calls upon us to walk a new walk and to talk a new talk. It insists that we face ourselves and others openly and with a view to change. Threatening, because a truly open man or woman exposes the sham and pretense in others, not so much by what is said as by the quality of their freedom. Thus a free person becomes easy prey for detractors.

Jesus suggests to us today that we struggle to find the right, equip ourselves to do the right, and ever persevere in the right. In spite of what others think or feel, Jesus says, Be free.

When we have been assisted in seeing the potential of the real self, we have a standard by which we can judge ourselves. It is likely that had Jesus not invited himself to be a guest at Zacchaeus' home, Zacchaeus would have continued to view life from uninvolved tree limbs.

Zacchaeus was forced to deal with himself and he saw life differently. His life came into sharper focus. The scales came off his eyes and he was able to say in effect: Jesus, you're O.K. You have stood me on my feet. You have given me vision of what life can hold. You have helped me know and understand myself. Hey, Jesus, you are truly O.K.

Now, because you're O.K., I'm O.K. I've done some things that were not right. I've cheated and stolen to accumulate my riches. Because you're O.K., I'm O.K. Therefore, if I have cheated anyone, I will pay him back fourfold.

This is what happens when we begin to march to the beat of a caring and consistent drummer. We have a standard by which to judge our lives. We come to understand and appreciate our own freedom and we seek that same freedom for others.

Because Jesus is O.K., we can be O.K. We can know the joy of being accepted. We can know what it means to affirm each other and not condemn. We can shout out our happiness over our society and be involved in the deepest fabric of that society. As black men and women we can fight to eradicate the racism in our midst and not become like that which we seek to change. We can joyously witness to what Christ has done for us. When we are loved we are capable of loving. When we encounter involvement we know how to get involved. When we experience forgiveness we can internalize and live out forgiveness. We learn by what we see and by what we do.

Jesus said to Zacchaeus, "Today salvation has come to your house." No greater salvation can any man have than to experience the love and acceptance of Jesus Christ. Jesus, *You're O.K.* Therefore, *I'm O.K.*

19
Sins of the Fathers

SHELBY ROOKS
St. James Presbyterian Church
New York, New York

Those who know Shelby Rooks agree unanimously that he has
mastered the art of sermon preparation and delivery. He and William
Lloyd Imes have made the pulpit of St. James Presbyterian Church
one of the outstanding preaching stations in the Northeast.

For thirty-three years parishioners and friends have listened to
Shelby Rooks's preaching. During this period black and white
seminarians have found him to be a model of homiletical craftsman-
ship. "Sins of the Fathers" reflects the incisiveness, vividness, and
balance of Rooks's preaching.

His pastoral record contains an interdenominational note. It is
occasioned by the fact that Rooks has pastored churches of the
Baptist, Congregational (United Church of Christ), and Presbyterian
denominations.

Rooks served a church in Brooklyn, New York, before going to St.
James, and sometime earlier he taught English Bible and homiletics
at Lincoln University in Pennsylvania. He had planned to retire from
the pastorate in August, but members of the congregation urged him
to extend his retirement date to December 31, 1976.

SERMON 19

The word of the Lord came unto me again, saying, What mean ye, that ye use this proverb concerning the land of Israel, saying, The fathers have eaten sour grapes, and the children's teeth are set on edge? As I live, saith the Lord God, ye shall not have occasion anymore to use this proverb in Israel.

EZEKIEL 18:1–3

From the time of Moses, the idea had gone unchallenged that the sins of the fathers are visited upon their children unto the third and fourth generations. In fairness to the great lawgiver, it should be recalled that the virtues of the fathers are also included in their legacy.

But in Ezekiel's day, as in ours, many of the old claims were being questioned. This was one of them. In a reasonable world, why should a son suffer for what his father did? The father lived his life; the son must claim the same right. What the old man did was his affair. The child may insist upon a like prerogative. This new message Ezekiel is trying to get over to the new age. And yet even he seems to doubt the soundness of this novel claim. All through this eighteenth chapter he keeps repeating this unfermented assertion. The reader is justified in concluding that Ezekiel never does resolve the matter to his own satisfaction.

And little wonder. Unreasonable it may seem, but the past does cling to us. The clay of the pit from which we were dug is deucedly hard to wash off. Long before the pretensions of modern geneticists were thought of, it was clear that the child was often a mirror image of the parent. Some of us grew up hearing it said that such and such a lad was "the spittin' image of his daddy."

There would appear to be nothing wrong with appeal to

one's own experience in a matter of this sort. My father, in his
grave these forty years, will be around as long as I live, for not
a day passes that I, in the looking glass or by a chance turn of
speech or a fragment of memory, am not made to acknowledge
that he is very much alive in me. Wouldn't you suppose that
a father, once buried, would be done for? Ezekiel's speculations
point to that conclusion. He is trying to get rid of the old
notion that if the father eats sour grapes his children's teeth
are set on edge. But even in the prophet's own mind there
seems to be a lingering concession that maybe Moses had
something. What if he was right: The sins of the fathers are
visited upon the children?

All of this is suggested by something I saw recently in a
two-page magazine spread calling attention to the highlights of
our American history over the past two centuries: Washington
crossing the Delaware; the Founding Fathers charting the
future in Philadelphia; Lincoln delivering his Second Inaugu-
ral; the Wright Brothers at Kitty Hawk; Lindbergh spanning
the Atlantic; the first moon landing. Then a closer look in
search of what was being offered to reflect the civil rights
struggle. Sure enough, there it was—federal troops protecting
the Little Rock black children as they entered a school that had
previously been open only to white youngsters. There was
nothing to suggest that Martin Luther King had ever lived.
And the reader could never have guessed, studying that picture
from sunrise to sunset on the longest day of summer, how those
troops, guns drawn, got there. They might have been, for all
that picture revealed, God-fearing volunteers shielding with
their lives innocent black boys and girls from evil of some
purely local and passing quarrel.

Here was clear proof that there is a whole lot of American
history of which this nation is ashamed; that we are not ready
to come to grips with the more gruesome truths of our past;
that every feast we spread is marred by a spectral presence. Our
long-ago trafficking in human flesh, attended by unwordable
degradation, is still a nightmare to recall. This went on, not like
the Nazi madness for a mere six years, but was done openly for

more than two centuries, and by practically the whole of Western Europe. The Jews lament the loss under the iron will of Hitler of an estimated six million. The number of victims of the Atlantic slave trade has never been calculated. White people often express wonder that there should be on the part of the Negro so much of what seems to them blind hatred and bitterness. But what else could be expected? Their fathers sowed the wind; the children are now reaping the whirlwind.

It can scarcely be surprising that the thoughtful black person wants nothing more than an arm's-length relationship with such a proven and intransigent foe. Even the white man's religion is suspect. Even on Sunday, if, as rarely happened, he found himself in the same church, the same pew, though not able always to put his finger on the precise reason, the black Christian never was able to throw off suspicion that he was somehow being had. The ludicrous apology occasionally offered by pious white Christians that slavery was God's inscrutable way of bringing the African to Jesus made matters worse. A Savior who could provide no better means of making himself known to the lost was scarcely worth knowing.

So it must be hard to plan a birthday party and invite friends from around the world, when so much of the past has to be passed over in embarrassed silence. The more so when it is remembered that we began with unprecedentedly lofty pretensions. Did we not set out to be a laboratory in human relations? Were we not bent on showing the world that man is endowed with certain inalienable rights? And underlying all was the conviction that a just God was in command of this experiment; that evil, once done, must somehow be redressed; that a generation unable to balance its moral ledger has no choice but to pass its liabilities on to its sons and daughters. Such remorse of conscience America has borne these two hundred years. The toll has been heavy in petulance and inner conflict.

From other lands visitors have often come, looking us over and wondering at the gap between what we say and what we do. Some openly doubted our ability to go on traveling in opposite directions toward one announced goal. Judgment has been offered politely or bluntly; but it comes to the same verdict. We are accused of trying to tote water on both shoulders. A long time ago, the British actress Fanny Kemble, horrified by what she saw of human bondage in the South, gave America a piece of her mind. The French statesman, De Tocqueville, saw much to admire and much to question. In our own century Gunnar Myrdal frankly describes our plight as a dilemma from which we may never emerge. James Pope-Hennessy has published a history of the slave trade, calling it, just as though he never heard of Ezekiel, *The Sins of the Fathers.*

There are sordid things in this nation's history, so sordid as to make one ashamed, almost, of being human. Would wild beasts do some of the things that come to light as we study our past?

It is sheer slander to suggest that these cruelties were suffered unresistingly by the defenseless captives. In chains and without weapons, where they could they fought back. They plotted rebellions, often murdering whole families in their beds. Life under such a yoke some found unendurable, throwing themselves into the sea in the course of the Middle Passage. Often, in impotent rage, they went raving mad.

So, this has to be one of the blood-chilling episodes in the whole grand and shabby sweep of the annals of humankind on this planet. It spotlights our tarnished motives and raises cynical doubts as to our self-deceiving moral posturings. It appears to nail down unanswerably the Biblical claim that the love of money is the root of all evil. When Queen Elizabeth was told of the first expedition being formed by her subjects for the purpose of raiding the West African coast to capture and enslave natives for sale in the West Indies, she flew into a rage. The idea that her Christian subjects should do such a swinish thing! But months later, when the expedition returned to report fabulous profits, Her Majesty expressed regret that she had passed up the chance to have a hand in such a blue-chip investment. She ordered forthwith a new expedition; this time she was in it up to here.

The slavers represented nearly all the maritime nations of Europe: England, Portugal, Spain, Holland, France. Once the flow of captives got started, this trading in human flesh became a grand design that lasted for centuries. And mind you, every one of these nations flaunted the Christian label—crucifixes in every home, churches on every hillside. These plunderers often professed feelings of piety. Their daily routine included morning prayers and Bible study. If such mockery can be imagined, they even told the story of Jesus to the slaves. It is enough to make one vomit. To this day, the descendants of black bondsmen are often rendered speechless and morbid by even passing mention of these reminders of the earliest contacts between Europeans and Africans. In the black slums of this land, rural and urban, this is not regarded as an album of past horrors. It is a hovering presence still, undated, ungranulated, giving no sign of eventual healing. Robert Burns has said that:

> Man's inhumanity to man
> Makes countless thousands mourn!

It certainly does, in this matter at least, make countless thousands hate. The familiar rubric, "Send no money now; you'll be billed later," suggests an aspect of our national experience. The slave trade in its original form we no longer have. But what a bill we are getting years later in terms of domestic conflict and mutual ill will. *The fathers ate sour grapes, and the children's teeth are set on edge.*

All of this deepens the anguish of the thoughtful Negro Christian. That there is a legacy of calm and considered hatred lodged in the very navel of many a black person in America should surprise nobody. That this detestation, often vented on Saturday night on other blacks, would under other circumstances be broken over stringy white heads, is written in the script, and must be accepted as human and natural. And yet the man or woman, black or white, who professes to move even at the periphery of Jesus' circle cannot settle for these facts, however stubborn and inevitable they may be. The soapbox tribune on 125th Street in Harlem, the black caucus in Washington, the civil rights leader haranguing his following in convention assembled—all these are perfectly free to select the facts that promote their special, sometimes self-serving, designs. They even have a fancy word now that cloaks such behavior: pragmatic.

But is that option open to the Christian, black or white? To revert to the text, if I insist on talking to the white man about the sins of his fathers, am I not bound to go on asking about the legacy handed down to me by my father? Master and slave may not operate by the same rules or employ the same techniques. Each will meet the exigencies of a given moment with such resources as are immediately available. However, it cannot be conceded, without lasting harm to my human fiber, that there are reaches of integrity permanently beyond my grasp simply because of my status in terms of color or condition. If I find myself in the house of God, it is degrading to me not to be able to do more than thank God that I am not as other men are. Not before I remember the sins of my own forebears should I demand that my white brother remember his. And if we are talking about the slave trade, God knows there is a lot on the black side that needs confessing. Were not the first enslavers of blacks themselves black? Did not the most stubborn resistance to the cessation of the trade come from the native chieftains who had been, so to say, "cleaning up" on what can only be described as a racket? It does not bother me that politicians don't openly say these things. What does bother me is my reluctance to speak the whole truth when I, like the Pharisee, go up to the temple to pray.

How is it, I wonder, that I am more tolerant of the exploitation, the filth, the disease, the beggary as I recall a brief visit I once made to Ethiopia than I am of what I have heard of human misery in South Africa? Has it anything to do with the fact that black men are the exploiters in one country, white men in the other? From the standpoint of what should be dominant in my mind when I find myself in church, should I not be ashamed of making such a distinction?

John Newton was a slaver out of England, but he had a

change of heart, converted to Christianity, and went on to a fruitful career as an evangelist. Centuries later, in our own time, Malcolm X, after many profligate years, mended his ways and sought to make his life count for good. Why is it that I find the former story harder to believe than the latter? Is the difference mainly this: that Newton was white, Malcolm black?

One hears tales of how Jefferson and his mulatto slave, Sally, carried on for years, begetting a considerable progeny. I find myself taking cheap shots at the master of Monticello, even insinuating that he should be discredited and unmasked as a deceiver. On the other hand, Du Bois, if we are to take his own word, as an old man looking back claimed to have been lifelong a discreet womanizer, but that never demeaned him in my eyes as a passionate spokesman for his people.

It is also remembered to Jefferson's discredit that he held on to his slaves, even while professing to agonize over this denial of principles he so eloquently set down on paper. I find it harder to forgive him than the blacks who were slaveholders. I wonder why.

The Negro who today tries to hold on to such tattered remains of the Christian faith as may be available to him is the prey of protean temptation. With dark and angry waters of resentment building against the white man for generations, he feels that he has something of a duty to identify with his black brothers, knowing of course that a religion of race has no more business in a house of worship than an exhibition of pornography can claim space in the Metropolitan Museum of Art. He must be on guard against being taken in by the black adventurer on the make who has no intention of asking any question more profound than, What's in it for me? A recent biographer of John Milton, commenting on the fact that the poet's reputation has held steady through three centuries, accounts for this massive character in part in these words: "He made his own character an issue in the public causes for which he fought." The Negro Christian must not allow himself to be taken over by any adventurer who is not willing to subscribe to this high standard.

But possibly it is from another quarter that the real temptation threatens. There was once a fiction that "colored folks" are naturally religious, that nothing could shake us from old moorings. That may have to go the way of a good many other specious claims about us. For scarcely behind others of the Western world, we are discovering ourselves to be praying in a universe that seems to have lost most of its resonance. Wouldn't it be a pity if we found ourselves, those of us who still go to church, just "making out" with the race question, thanking God that we are not as other men are?

20
From Babel to Pentecost

JOHN GATU
All-Africa Conference of Churches
Kenya, East Africa

The official report of the Third Assembly of the All-Africa Confer-ence of Churches contains this statement: John Gatu "held the entire congregation spellbound by his powerful thought-provoking sermon." This reference attests to the homiletical ability of this African preacher.

Some preachers possess the skill of making a sermon sound good. However, in cold print they do not read well. This is not true of Gatu's sermons. They are well written and are effectively presented.

Gatu is a consistent and convincing advocate for the "self-hood of the church" in the Third World. His speeches, sermons, and articles reflect a strong commitment to "challenge those who are colonizing those who are unable to defend and liberate themselves."

John Gatu is the chairperson of the General Committee of the All-Africa Conference of Churches. This position gives him the op-portunity of providing dedicated leadership to the members of the Conference. Also, it provides us with the privilege of hearing God speak to us through an articulate servant of the Presbyterian Church of East Africa.

SERMON 20

When Pentecost day came round, they had all met in one room, when suddenly they heard what sounded like a powerful wind from heaven, the noise of which filled the entire house in which they were sitting; and something appeared to them that seemed like tongues of fire; these separated and came to rest on the head of each of them. They were all filled with the Holy Spirit, and began to speak foreign languages as the Spirit gave them the gift of speech.

ACTS 2:1–4 (JERUSALEM BIBLE)

Today in the church calendar we celebrate the Sunday after Ascension. I have felt, however, strongly persuaded to speak about the celebration of the pouring of the Holy Spirit to the church, the occasion which we should be celebrating next Sunday according to our church calendar. I am doing this because I believe that Pentecost does have more than a religious significance to man today than we normally think. It is for this reason that I like calling the title of this sermon "From Babel to Pentecost."

Let us first of all recall the story of the Tower of Babel. In the early days of education in this country, boys and girls who lived in dormitories on mission compounds were known in the Kikuyu language as *mambere* or *andu a mambere*. I am told there are two explanations as to how these terms came about. (1) That in the evenings after the lights were put out in the dormitories and boys were all ordered to sleep, normally there ensued a lot of talking, sometimes very loud. Because no one could understand much of what was being talked about— maybe the pupils understood each other, but teachers could not—the dormitory came to be equated with the Tower of Babel. (2) That because people living in those dormitories acted on the sound of the bell—for their meals, breaks, etc.— the name then came to be adopted as People of the Bell, *mambere.* I am more inclined to believe the former than the latter.

The story of the Tower of Babel in our Bible not only shows us how different languages came into being, but it also shows us the judgment of God on all those who try to exalt themselves above God. These people were nomads migrating from the desert into the fertile and cultivated valley of Babylonia, where they settled. They were very conscious of their own security and wanted to ensure it in every possible way. They feared to be scattered all over the world, they said. Therefore, out of pride, fear, and antagonism against God they decided to build this high tower whose top would reach heaven. In fact, they were so self-confident that instead of using stones, which would have been more permanent, they used bricks. They did not hide their intention, namely, that they wanted to *make themselves a name.* This is not unlike the arms struggle that we find among the big nations of the world today. The smaller nations cannot be excused from the same wish in many other ways. But the Bible, and especially the story of the Tower of Babel, teaches us that where man's aim is to glorify himself and his achievements, the end result is confusion, for that is what "Babel" means. And eventually he loses the same security that he wishes to retain for himself. History is full of examples of nations and empires that built "towers" which became symbols of ruthless power and oppression. The story continues to say that although these people wished the tower to reach heaven, eventually it is God who came down to see the tower.

Our own achievement cannot bring us any nearer to God, but it is God who first takes the initiative to visit us, and unless we admit our pride, our selfishness, and our utter inadequacy before the sight of God, we are then scattered and confused. Now we turn to Pentecost.

PENTECOST. If the confusion in the Tower of Babel had been all that God could do for man, he would not have been the kind of God to whom I would like to pledge my allegiance.

He would be the God of destruction, chaos, and confusion. But I thank God that there was and there is a Pentecost. That is where the story of the Tower of Babel is so completely reversed.

1. Although those who gathered in Jerusalem—i.e., the disciples—were, like the builders of the Tower of Babel, of one mind, it was a different kind of mind. People can be united in doing a bad or a good thing and still claim this to be democratic. In the case of the disciples, however:

a. They were united by their awareness of their total inadequacy for the task before them after their Lord had ascended to heaven. They needed strength.

b. They were under no illusion whatsoever about the inherent dangers they were likely to face. They needed to move and not to settle down.

c. They were in earnest expectation to receive the promise given them by their Lord for the coming of the Comforter, who will lead them into all truth.

Doesn't the Bible teach us that "where two or three are gathered together in my *name*, there am I in the midst of them"? The disciples were gathering in the *name of their Lord and God;* therefore God was in their midst. Those who built the Tower of Babel gathered in their *own name* to celebrate their own achievement and subsequently they expelled God from their midst—and confusion, therefore, ensued.

Back to Pentecost again. We are told that:

2. *There was a powerful wind from heaven.* This was the confirmation from God that he was in their midst, and that while his Son had actually ascended to heaven, he was not going to leave them without someone who will understand their needs, their concerns, and their human weaknesses: someone who understands the tremendous dangers that were facing them in their new mission and one who was going to see them through. Surely if Nicodemus had been present at Pentecost, he would have understood much more clearly the equation which was impossible for him to solve let alone understand

when he visited Jesus one night. Jesus had said, "The wind bloweth where it listeth, and thou hearest the sound thereof, but canst not tell whence it cometh . . . : so is every one that is born of the Spirit." This is now the coming of the Holy Spirit and the seal of the heavenly promise.

3. *It is the Spirit of strength.* You will remember the story of the disciples in chapter 20 of John's Gospel, when the disciples were almost hiding for fear of what might follow them after the death of Jesus. After Jesus had given them the promise of peace, which was undoubtedly the one thing they needed most, we read that he then "breathed on them, and saith unto them, Receive ye the Holy Ghost: whosesoever sins ye remit, they are remitted unto them; and whosesoever sins ye retain, they are retained." This was the strength, power, and authority that was going to accompany them wherever the Lord sent them. Henceforth, the cowards like Peter who could not stand the little girl at the night of betrayal can now stand up in the midst of a crowd of more than three thousand people; the doubting Thomas now has the strength and the power to say, I do not need to touch, *now I know.* They are not going in their own name but in the name of their Lord and God in Christ.

4. *Tongues of fire settled on each one of them.* While the room was filled with the Spirit, there were also tongues of fire that rested upon each one of those who were there. God deals with us not only collectively but also individually. While he is concerned with nations, whether these be big or small nations, he is also equally concerned with each individual, regardless of any status the individual has. Sometimes, when we commit certain sins we like to hide ourselves from other people and think we are hiding ourselves from God as well; or sometimes we may sin collectively as a group, and think we shall not be punished individually. The word of God remains true—*Your sin will find you out.*

5. *It was fire.* Man on his own is like a piece of unrefined gold, and so were the disciples, and those met in Jerusalem.

They certainly possessed great possibilities and potentials, but needed purging or refining. This is a very familiar Biblical concept which we also find in the Book of Isaiah when God revealed himself to the prophet and touched him with a piece of coal on his lips. The lips of the disciples needed a touch of fire to cleanse them. How much more do we need the same touch ourselves in Kenya so that we can speak words of love and concern for our fellowmen; words of unity and brotherhood so that we can preach the gospel instead of gossiping?

6. *They needed to be on fire for the good news.* If ever Christians needed to be on fire for the Lord, this is the time. For all over the world today there are divisive elements haunting the brotherhood of man. Man is therefore highly perplexed and in that situation he acts out of fear and not love. Our preaching is pointless unless it is endowed by the power of the Holy Spirit when we are on fire with him.

7. *It was the sign of our adoption.* Do you remember the hymn "Come, Holy Spirit, Come"? There is another verse that says "To pour fresh life in every part, and new-create the whole."

It is the Holy Spirit who creates us anew when we become sons and daughters of his kingdom. Consequently, we become brothers and sisters to each other. Instead of our individualism, we become responsible beings.

In other words, when we are born again of the Spirit of God, not only do we become responsible to God in the sense that we are answerable to him but we also become responsible to and for our fellowmen as trustees of that which belongs to us all. This is why a Christian should not engage in dirty business tricks even though he knows very well that this would give him quick money; that is why a Christian will treat kindly an orphan or a widow and endeavor to help those who cannot otherwise help themselves without asking for a bribe, because he is responsible to God and responsible for his brother. In this sense, he is right and correctly *his brother's keeper,* a responsibility given to him by the nature of his being a child of God.

We must all realize that we stand before an infinite judge and creator who is never deceived by our human craftiness.

8. *The wind was an awakening.* Man, in his normal character, likes to take it easy. You remember the disciples who went with Jesus to Gethsemane, while he was praying for the cup of death to be taken from him? Jesus comes to them three times and each time he finds them asleep. Can you not watch with me for just one hour? Jesus asks them. The disciples were not sensitive to the dangers around. Man can be very insensitive. We can all fail to read the signs of the time or the writing on the wall in the same way. We therefore need the Holy Spirit to wake us up from self-complacency and pride. We need to be awakened to the needs of Kenya today; the needs of East Africa; the needs of the world and its future, so that each one of us can play his rightful part in bringing a spirit of Pentecost to us all.

9. *It was a disturbing wind.* The Holy Spirit is expected not only to comfort but also to disturb the rest of the world. At Pentecost, people were disturbed. They thought that the disciples were a bunch of drunkards, drunk with the newest brand of wine. In Kenya today we might probably say, they were drunk with *chang'aa.* One of the great phenomena of our times in Kenya today is the religious revival currently sweeping across the nation. It can be seen in the building of churches, in church attendances, in the zeal for evangelism among young people and students; but perhaps much more than anything else, in the composition of religious songs arising from personal and individual convictions and faith in God. Numerous hymn-books have been published, and for the first time we are beginning to see the power of the Holy Spirit expressed in drums, musical instruments, and tunes composed by local people using cultural expressions which mean much more than any translations from English or German hymns and songs which we have been singing for more than seventy years. Listen to them carefully and you will discover a prophetic message for today. We must praise God for this spirit.

10. Perhaps the most important aspect of Pentecost, which I have not mentioned so far, was the breaking of the language barrier first experienced at the Tower of Babel.

The need to provide human understanding, the need to listen to each other, the gift of knowing what would annoy your brother and therefore avoiding it, the breaking of cultural barriers—these and many others have never been more urgent and greater in our world. God has now come down, not as he did at Babel to confuse, but in the power of his Holy Spirit to improve human relationships and reconcile man to his Creator. If you ask me what is the need for us in Kenya today, for East Africa and indeed the world, I would quickly answer you and say, An experience of Pentecost. By this I do not mean specifically what some people think is the only proper manifestation of the baptism of the Holy Spirit, namely, speaking with tongues. For Paul has reminded us, "If I speak in the tongues of men and of angels, but have not love, I am a noisy gong or a clanging cymbal."

But it is to wish and to pray that, all of us, whether we belong to church or not, whether in business or in the civil service, whether employers or employees, educated or uneducated, taking into account whatever other differences may exist within our society and nation—that we should not adopt the spirit of Babel, i.e., the spirit of personal exhortation or pride of personal achievements without the fear of God, but in fear and trembling we should all accept our utter inadequacy before God; accept valid criticisms; accept our human failings and the need to be given that power of love and concern which was poured onto the disciples. The spirit that would give a new sense of direction; the spirit that would accept our commonality, our collective as well as individual responsibility to this land, to each other, and above all to God himself. The spirit of "love, joy, peace, patience, kindness, generosity, fidelity, tolerance, and self-control—and no law exists against any of them" (Gal. 5:20, Phillips), so that when the voice of God comes to us as it came to Cain of old, "Where is Abel, your brother?" instead of answering, "I know not; am I my brother's keeper?" you and I would very happily answer, "I know where my brother is: I am my brother's keeper because he is my keeper also."

21

Blackness as Sign and Assignment

GAYRAUD S. WILMORE
Colgate Rochester Theological Seminary
Rochester, New York

Effective teacher, prolific writer, articulate exponent of black theology, extensive traveler, effective preacher—these phrases reflect
some of the gifts and talents of Gayraud Wilmore. They also reveal
why this Martin Luther King, Jr., Professor of Black Studies at
Colgate Rochester Theological Seminary is in frequent demand as
seminar leader, lecturer, and preacher.

Gayraud Wilmore was born in Philadelphia, Pennsylvania. His
high school, college, and seminary training were received in Pennsylvania.

After graduation from the seminary of Lincoln University in Ches-
ter County, Pennsylvania, he served as pastor of Second Presbyterian
Church, West Chester, Pennsylvania, for three years. This was fol-
lowed by a three-year stint as Regional Secretary of the Student
Christian Movement. Some of his other professional experiences are:
Assistant Secretary, Department of Social Education and Action,
Board of Christian Education, The United Presbyterian Church in
the United States of America; assistant professor of social ethics,
Pittsburgh Theological Seminary; director of the Council on Church
and Race, The United Presbyterian Church in the United States of
America; and professor of social ethics, Boston University.

Dr. Wilmore is the author of two books: *Black Religion and Black
Radicalism* and *The Secular Relevance of the Church.* Many of his
articles have been published in journals and magazines in this country
and overseas.

"Blackness as Sign and Assignment" is a sample of the right insight
regarding the black experience that Gayraud Wilmore gives his read-
ers and listeners. His is one of the clearest voices on the current
liberation theology theme. This sermon is one indication why.

Son of man, you dwell in the midst of a rebellious house. . . . Therefore, . . . prepare for yourself an exile's baggage, . . . for I have made you a sign for the house of Israel.

EZEKIEL 12:2–3, 6

Many people are confused about blackness. The term is used in many different ways today and the result is that most of us are thoroughly confused. Black Power, Black Pride, Black Studies, Black Theology—what are we to make of blackness? Is the word nothing more than a kind of arbitrary synonym for Negro, colored, or Afro-American—or is there a more substantive meaning related to something eminently significant about us as a people? Let me put it another way: Is there a profound religious meaning in the idea of being a black people?

Let me put it squarely before you. I believe that black Christians—the black church in Africa and America—should articulate the theological meaning of blackness that arises from our religious experience as a people. I believe that we need to understand blackness as both a sign and an assignment from God.

I

Ezekiel is given a sign and an assignment from God. He had no choice in the matter. God didn't ask him if he would like to take on this assignment. He simply said: "Son of man, I have made you a watchman over the house of Israel. I am giving you a sign to take to these people. If you carry my sign and no one heeds it, they will be the worse for it, but you at least will be saved. If, on the other hand, you refuse to carry it and people do not get the message that I am sending to them, I am going to take out their punishment on you."

Ezekiel is asked to do a strange thing. He is to enact a kind of pantomime of the Babylonian exile. He is told by God to dress himself up like an exile, put an exile's baggage upon his shoulders, and go out through the city walls in the darkness of night, as one going sadly under great burden into captivity. In this way Ezekiel *himself* becomes a sign. He portrays a humiliated, captive people who have turned their backs upon their God and must suffer the consequence of being uprooted and driven out from the comfort and safety that God has given them. Ezekiel, with his exile's clothing and baggage, *was* God's message. He symbolized in his own being what God was saying to the people. He was not told to stand on the corner and preach this message. He was not asked to write and publish it. He had to leave his own home for a time, pack his belongings and put them on his back, dig through the city wall and go out into the blackness of night—"for I have made you," said God, "a sign for the house of Israel."

Let us substitute the color of blackness for the exile's clothing and for the baggage that Ezekiel carried by God's command. Certainly colors are used in all human societies as signs or symbols. From the most ancient and primitive people to our modern society, colors have been understood to convey powerful messages. The color symbolism of white Western societies has come, of course, to dominate most of the world. Wherever the white man has gone, his color symbolism—the assignment he has given to certain colors—has tended to become standard.

A simple example is the meaning of traffic signals. No matter where you are—in Hong Kong, Dar es Salaam, Santiago, or Atlanta—red means danger, yellow means caution, green means go. What about black and white? There is some ambiguity about these colors. But generally speaking, in Europe and America painting, literature, and cultural artifacts have conveyed the message that white symbolizes truth, beauty, purity, and goodness, while black symbolizes shame, impurity, ignorance, and evil.

Western symbolism—carried around the world by Western armies and missionaries—has made people believe that God himself decreed that "white is right, brown can stick around, but black must go back." More than that, according to this symbolism, God is white and Satan is black.

Did God authorize this symbolism? Of course not. Nor did black people authorize it. White men, by the sheer power of their culture—their money, guns, and Bibles—made this kind of white/black symbolism operative first in Europe and America, later in South Africa, and now all over the world. But just as the white man can make up his mind about the meaning of blackness and back it up by his interpretation of the will of God, we black people can change that meaning.

This is no idle matter. Colors convey powerful religious meanings, as the history of liturgics shows. And if a white preacher like the Rev. Buchner Payne can say that God chose whiteness because there is no darkness in him and that there can be no darkness in heaven, a black preacher can say that God chose blackness because God is mystery and cosmic fecundity, for there can be no white, lifeless sterility in heaven!

II

What I am really saying is that we black people have a right, even a responsibility, to interpret the Christian faith in such a way as to make blackness a profound expression of our religious experience. Even though black experience has usually been betrayal, suffering, and affliction, we can read the meaning of that experience in positive rather than negative terms, because of what we know about God and his relationship to those who trust in him.

One day men came and reported to Jesus about some Galileans who had fallen into Pilate's hands and had been killed. Luke does not tell us the questions they asked, but they probably had to do with whether Jesus thought this tragic event demonstrated the sinfulness of the victims. In other words, was this God's punishment for their sins? "No," said Jesus, "but the same thing could happen to you if you do not repent of yours!" On another occasion when the disciples passed by a man born blind they asked, "Rabbi, who sinned, this man or his parents, that he was born blind?" Jesus answered, "It was not that this man sinned, or his parents, but that the works of God might be made manifest in him."

The implication of both of these incidents is that God permits tragedy and hardships to come upon us for mysterious reasons of his own, not necessarily because we are offenders more than others. Indeed, he may even command some people to bear greater burdens than others in order that his will may be known. He summoned Ezekiel to bear the symbol of exile and captivity and sent him out into the darkness as a sign of what had been prepared for a rebellious people. While the false prophets lied about how much God was going to bless the people, Ezekiel dramatically portrayed the grim reality of their real situation.

Is there a lesson for us in Ezekiel's prophetic assignment? I believe so. In the face of man's false sense of security, in the face of his illusions about who he is and what he is able to accomplish by his own hands, in the face of his lies about truth and justice, blackness and the black experience of suffering and oppression stand as God's witness to reality, to the truth about life. Blackness is the way life *really* is. It is a sign of affliction and oppression, not of punishment and corruption. And there is a vast difference between the two that requires a complete revision of the color symbolism of Western culture. Blackness is indeed a symbol of what we have suffered, but we may bear it proudly not only because we have learned how to survive and sing the songs of Zion in a strange land, but because, like Ezekiel, God has called us in our blackness to bear a message to all people.

In *The Gift of Black Folk,* Du Bois speaks of the black presence in America as tragedy reflected in the sorrow songs or spirituals, but he saw in the black experience something that said a great deal about the vulnerability of all human existence, about the elemental nature of suffering and woe, about death as a natural and inevitable part of life. This is the message of blackness assigned by God himself. In a civilization that believes that all men can be sexually attractive and all women can be queens every day, in a culture where people hide from suffering and avert their eyes from the slums when they drive over them on thruways to suburbia, in a world that believes that man is the measure of all things and that human progress is inevitable, blackness is a religious symbol of a stern reality which continues to frustrate man's noblest designs, a reality which must be lived and experienced lest a people perish by their own fatuous illusions. The psalmist writes:

> Thou dost sweep men away . . .
>   like grass which is renewed in the morning:
> in the morning it flourishes and is renewed;
>   in the evening it fades and withers. . . .
> For all our days pass away under thy wrath,
>   our years come to end like a sigh.

Black people have always well understood those words. It is because of this understanding that we have learned to act like men and women of flesh and blood and to let only God be God. Like Paul we know how to be full and how to be empty. We know we live in a sinful, imperfect world and that emptiness is the portion given, soon or late, to all people. When we cry out in the midnight hour, "O Lord, have mercy on my soul!" it is because we know that life "ain't been no crystal stair" and "the higher you climb the harder you fall." God made life that way, and man can never change it.

Blackness is a beautiful sensitivity to the hard, tragic dimension in life—a part of living that everyone must learn to negotiate, because, whether rich or poor, famous or infamous, black or white, we are all pitiable, vulnerable human beings and we have to go down into the pit together. Blackness is a message to the world that a man's arm is too short to box with God;

that he is so high you can't get over him, so low you can't get under him, so wide you can't get around him—you must come in by the Door. And that Door is the door of trials and tribulation which is personified by Jesus. That Door is what makes a people both humble and strong. "Yet do I marvel at this curious thing: to make a poet black, and bid him sing."

III

. I have been talking about blackness as a symbol of perennial human condition. Blackness is also the message that man must struggle against every power that seeks to subdue and dehumanize him. Blackness symbolizes the truth that even though you may be down, you are not necessarily out. And by God's grace you will rise again.

Jesus Christ is crucial to black Christianity because darkness was his experience, and we know something about darkness. The Good Friday spiritual asks the question, "Were you there?" And the unspoken answer is, "Yes, we were all there when the Nigger of Galilee was lynched in Jerusalem." Is there any wonder that we can identify with him?

Black people, whether in America or in Africa, know Jesus as the Oppressed Man of God, who fraternized with harlots and sinners, who helped the poor and lowly, who struggled against the powers of evil in church and state, who was crucified in apparent defeat. We, of all the people of the world, can identify with that story because that is precisely what blackness has meant for us—lowliness, struggle, and defeat. Like Jesus on the cross, we too have cried out against the darkness in our flesh and in our environment, "My God, my God, why have you forsaken us?"

But as Jesus stood the test, we too stood the test, singing our blues and gospel, finger-popping all the while. As his strength was made perfect in weakness, so was ours. We never stopped struggling against the powers of oppression, poverty, and racism, and I believe we never will, because we have learned from Jesus that life itself is a struggle, and if you can't stand the heat, you will never be able to work in the kitchen. "In the world you have tribulation; but be of good cheer, I have overcome the world."

Blackness, therefore, is God's message through us to all people that to resist, to struggle, to wrestle, fight, and pray—and yet laugh and sing and "get happy"—is what it means to be a human being. Human beings know how to love and have compassion and get along with people in this world.

We do indeed have enemies and we have by no means conquered them within or without. But we continue to struggle with hope because we believe that even in death we shall be victorious through the Oppressed Son of God who conquered death, even death on the cross. That is why, as strange as it may sound in a world dominated by Western symbolism, we can speak of Jesus as our Black Messiah, because in so doing we chain ourselves not only to his cross but to his resurrection from defeat; we make blackness the sign and symbol not only of his struggle but also of his glorious victory which we will share.

IV

My final word is that we have little choice but to be God's sign and live, or refuse to be God's sign and die as a people. We did not ask to be born in this color, nor did we choose the slavery, suffering, and humiliation against which we have been struggling all these years. But neither did Ezekiel have a choice when God called him in Tel-abib to bear witness to the meaning of the Babylonian captivity. The only choice he had, or that we have, is how we shall interpret the meaning of our individual and corporate lives. Only a religious meaning, only a religious interpretation of our pilgrimage, can satisfy the deepest yearnings of our hearts.

How, then, shall we understand blackness? As an accident of history in a world of absurdity and meaninglessness? As a curse and a punishment? Or as a profound and mysterious assignment from God by which we have been called to bear witness to the message of his judgment and his grace to all the nations of the world and especially to white America?

In a nation where blackness and oppression have seemed inseparable, my faith will permit no other answer than that God has made my people a sign to an arrogant, self-aggrandizing, rebellious generation. He has commanded us to say to the world: "This is *your* life too. This is what it means to be human —to suffer, to struggle, to fight with hope against the powers of hell—to die and to be raised victorious with Jesus Christ. Therefore, take heed of us and live!"

It is the responsibility of the black church to preserve this black image of humanity against all the whitenizing acids of the modern age. Young black men and women of this generation, do not forsake the rock from which you were hewn to choose an easier but less challenging road on which to travel. Give your heart, mind, and will to God. Return to the black church and to reality, to humanity and to struggle, to the assignment of your blackness. For God has not left himself without a witness in this evil day. As he said to the prophet Ezekiel, so he continues to say, "Son of man, you dwell in the midst of a rebellious house. . . . Therefore, . . . prepare for yourself an exile's baggage, . . . for I have made you a sign for the house of Israel." God has made us a sign of judgment, grace, and love. Let all who have eyes to see, see and believe in the struggle and the victory through Jesus Christ, our crucified and risen Lord.

INDEX